BEYOND THE DRIFT

David Scott was born in 1947 in Cambridge. He was educated at Solihull School, and studied Theology at Durham and then at Cuddesdon College near Oxford. He spent two years as a curate in Harlow, and then became School Chaplain at Haberdashers' Aske's School, Elstree, where he taught religious education. He was vicar of Torpenhow and Allhallows in Cumbria, and in 1991 moved to Winchester to become rector of St Lawrence with St Swithun-upon-Kingsgate. Canon Scott retired in September 2010 and now lives in Cumbria. He is an Honorary Canon of Winchester Cathedral and an honorary fellow of the University of Winchester. In 2008 the Archbishop of Canterbury conferred on David Scott a Lambeth Degree Doctorate of Letters (DLitt).

In 1978 David Scott won the *Sunday Times*/BBC national poetry competition with his poem 'Kirkwall Auction Mart'. His first book of poems, *A Quiet Gathering* (Bloodaxe Books, 1984), won him the Geoffrey Faber Memorial Prize in 1986. His second collection, *Playing for England* (Bloodaxe Books, 1989) was a Poetry Book Society Recommendation. Both books were illustrated by Graham Arnold of the Brotherhood of Ruralists. The poems from those two collections were republished with new work in his *Selected Poems* (Bloodaxe Books, 1998), and followed by *Piecing Together* in 2005. David Scott's latest book, *Beyond the Drift: New & Selected Poems* (Bloodaxe Books, 2014), draws on his four previous Bloodaxe titles, with the addition of a whole collection of new poems.

David Scott's collection of poems for children, *How Does It Feel?* was published by Blackie in 1989. He has also written several plays for the National Youth Music Theatre with Jeremy James Taylor. These include *Captain Stirrick*, which was staged at the National Theatre's Cottesloe Theatre in 1981; *Bendigo Boswell*, which was commissioned by the BBC and screened in 1983; and *The Powder Monkeys* (1993). *Jack Spratt VC* was performed in the 1986 London International Opera Festival, and *Les Petits Rats* was performed at the Edinburgh International Festival and Sadlers Wells in 1988.

He has published six books on religious subjects, *Moments of Prayer* (SPCK, 1997), *Building Common Faith* (Canterbury Press, 1997), *An Anglo-Saxon Passion* (SPCK, 1999), *Sacred Tongues: The Golden Age of Spiritual Writing* (SPCK, 2001), *Lancelot Andrewes: The Private Prayers* (SPCK, 2002), and *The Mind of Christ* (Continuum, 2006).

DAVID SCOTT

BEYOND THE DRIFT
NEW & SELECTED POEMS

BLOODAXE BOOKS

ISBN: 978 1 78037 104 7

First published 2014 by
Bloodaxe Books Ltd,
Eastburn,
South Park,
Hexham,
Northumberland NE46 1BS.

www.bloodaxebooks.com
For further information about Bloodaxe titles
please visit our website and join our mailing list
or write to the above address for a catalogue

Supported using public funding by
**ARTS COUNCIL
ENGLAND**

Cover design: Neil Astley & Pamela Robertson-Pearce.

Digital reprint of the 2014 Bloodaxe Books edition.

For Miggy

ACKNOWLEDGEMENTS

The poems in the first four sections of this edition are reprinted from the following books by David Scott, all published by Bloodaxe Books: *A Quiet Gathering* (1984), *Playing for England* (1989), *Selected Poems* (1998) and *Piecing Together* (2005); the new poems in the fifth section are previously uncollected.

'The Cuff-links and the Cockermouth Floods' was published in *The Cockermouth Poets 1700-2012*, edited by Michael Baron and Joan Hetherington (Octogenary Press, 2012).

CONTENTS

from **PLAYING FOR ENGLAND** (1989)

from **SELECTED POEMS** (1998)

from PIECING TOGETHER (2005)

BEYOND THE DRIFT: NEW POEMS (2014)

from

A QUIET GATHERING

(1984)

Kirkwall Auction Mart

There are no bolts that do not exactly
fit the gates into and out of the store-ring.
Hundreds of times a day the same slamming iron
marshals cattle lots, hooves fighting the sand,
until the stick smacks them into view.
A nod decides the hidden bidders
and for these ghosts a litany is sung
bridging the jump in bids by the ancient
rattling of tongues until a bashed hand settles it.
Paper slips locate the buyers. We might
have guessed it would be a man of dull cloth,
hunched over the front rail, his smoke
joining the wreath of snorted breath high up
in the roof, who knew his business, and bought.

Illness

Hers was the vacant seat by the door.
To choose the nearest was her way of coping
with the recent bother of always feeling tired,
especially today, with the sudden change in weather.
At first, the shopping basket held her up,
but sleep soon capsized her
to the angle a holed tanker is towed at.
I wondered if the illness would come as a surprise
to her, leaving the family to shop for muddled meals;
and how she would wake up eventually;
by a kindly tap at the end of the line,
or in panic, not sure of the stop.

Venus

Behind a counter, she was offering silks
and bells in the perfumed air.
Each mirror had its own angle
came up with its own tender zone
of elbow, press of the crown of hair,
tilting foot, nape of neck.
I could see why she was chosen
for Venus. It was summer
when all sorts of things can happen.
Let her be Venus for a while,
until the first hard winter
rings the bell of the boutique behind her.

Leavesden Asylum, 1880

All the apparatus is well made.
The deathcart for example has its canvas
tight on the wood, and the wheels turn straight.
Even the certificates are stylishly printed
on fine paper fit for the Master's signature.
The rules are numbered and in bold print,
defining the length of visits, and formalising
a whole range of separations; stamping out
the illicit gift pressed into the palm
before the hour when the gate is locked
and the authorities will not be roused.
The architects had as many bricks as they required,
and since none would admire it, the blocks
could use up the sky, with each ward
the precise dimension of all the others.
The window sills are high enough to hold up
a face vacant as bread for a hand to wave at
from the yard. February is cold except
for a bed's length from the stove. August,
too hot for a canvas dress and black, lace-up boots.

Letters from Baron Von Hügel to a Niece

His day was not really complete until
he sealed with a gentle middle finger
a letter to his niece, heralding the arrival
of books. It smelt of camphor. The advice
was a comfort to her: 'Give up Evensong,
and even if dying never strain.'
It was surprising counsel from one so scrupulous;
whose sharp pencil noted on both margins of a page,
and hovered, like a teacher's, over spelling.
Walking into Kensington with the letter,
his muffler tight against the frost,
he reassures himself that directing a soul
is not only a matter of angel's talk, it is
also the knack of catching the evening post.

For John Ball

Travelling from Durham on the early train
we would arrive without warning, and in no time,
you half into your cassock, there would be coffee.
If there was no reply, then either you were tired
of passing traffic; or were saying mass in church,
which was reached from the square with the plane trees
through a parish of tenements and seedy hotels.
Your other parish was us. We came to you
because like your favourite poet Stevie Smith
you sat still; and had a private voice
which only carried as far as it needed.
News of your death came as no surprise.
I sensed that one day I would turn up
and you would not be able to rise, tiny priest,
on the one, strong, slender hand that did for two.

Queen's Park, Glasgow

They came separately hoping for a game
but passing the all-weather tennis court
sagging with pools of rain, it did not look hopeful.
The man in the pitch-and-put cabin
looked dismally out at the two lads
knocking wild balls at the last tin flag.
Soon he could go home. The bowlers put on
their brogues, as charms against the rain,
but one, not doing up his laces under the flap
knew it was no good, and nipping his cigarette,
said so. It was enough. The single file trailed round
the cinder path, macs covering blazers heavy
with the club badge; woods still snug with the jack.

Groundsmen

The pile of cuttings puts on dreadful weight,
swelters in the season, and leaks treacle.
Beside it, the tractor and the cutters drip oil
into the earth floor, in a shed where cobwebs
link the roof to the wired window and the oil drums.
The twisted blades and the spiked roller
rest from the nibbling and pricking of the pitch;
and in the corner a white liner, clogged white
round the wheels, darkens towards the handles.
The quiet men whose stuff this is
have the next shed along. Their door shuts
neatly to, unlike the tractor shed
where the door drags and billows against the bricks.
It was a secret kingdom for a boy.
I envied them their work; lending out bats,
lowering the posts, the twirl of the cutter
at the end of a straight run; and their shed
at the edge of the known world.

A Long Way from Bread

1

We have come so far from bread.
Rarely do we hear the clatter of the mill wheel;
see the flour in every cranny,
the shaking down of the sack, the chalk on the door,
the rats, the race, the pool,
baking day, and the old loaves:
cob, cottage, plaited, brick.

We have come so far from bread.
Once the crock said 'BREAD'
and the bread was what was there,
and the family's arm went deeper down each day
to find it, and the crust was favoured.

We have come so far from bread.
Terrifying is the breach between wheat and table,
wheat and bread, bread and what goes for bread.
Loaves come now in regiments, so that loaf
is not the word. *Hlaf*
is one of the oldest words we have.

2

I go on about bread
because it was to bread
that Jesus trusted
the meaning he had of himself.
It was an honour for bread
to be the knot in the Lord's handkerchief
reminding him about himself. So,
O bread, breakable;
O bread, given;
O bread, a blessing;
count yourself lucky, bread.

3

Not that I am against wafers,
especially the ones produced under steam
from some hidden nunnery
with our Lord crucified into them.
They are at least unleavened, and fit the hand,
without remainder, but it is still
a long way from bread.
Better for each household to have its own bread,
daily, enough and to spare,
dough the size of a rolled towel,
for feeding angels unawares.
Then if the bread is holy,
all that has to do with bread is holy:
board, knife, cupboard,
so that the gap between all things is closed
in our attention to the bread of the day.

4

I know that
'man cannot live on bread alone'.
I say, let us get the bread right.

Flower Rota

The niche in the pillar
with its chance ledge
had been chosen
by two mothers jointly
for sons killed in action.

On Saturday, in memory
of the day their sons fell,
they arrange the flowers;
brush the fallen petals;
return the watering can
to the tap by the wall.

Early on the Sunday morning
they can see the solidago
shot with sun, atoning
for their death on the hill
that terrible April.

Poplar

At the heart
of the trembling poplar
is a leaf stalk, ribbed
and longer than the stalk itself
which is how the wind
can whisper its rumour
right across Lombardy.

The lopped trunks
spindle thin
like foals' legs
hold their scanning leaves
crisp as radar
decoding the sun.

The wood of the poplar tree
is used for matches, cart floors,
and around Jerusalem and Galilee
for crosses; which is why
the blood silver coppice
still shivers in remembrance.

Ash

The clumps of winter seeds
hang off the branch
like warders' keys;
those branches which
have ashed urchins.

The tough, close-grained wood
made shafts for spears.
At the Battle of Maldon
ash meant spear.

Take a leaf
and close it like a book;
being pinnate
it will couple perfectly.

I know it best
for the charcoal buds,
and the stick that won't snap;
only fracture, shred
with the twist, and hang limp.

Mud

The books call it
rich, friable loam,
but me and my son
say mud. See it hold the stream
like a farmer's palm.
Air gets at the iron
oxidising. All the same
we see rust
encouraging the frozen flame.
Take cold fistfuls,
like woad;
paint it on –
see how the hairs spring gold.

Canal

The canal is asleep with history.
It has eaten too much, and is stuck
between cemented locks. Its maw
packed with pram; bicycle frame;
tyres; springs; cooker; sun.
It has the quietness of courtyards.
Swans sleep the sun away; their
snouts in the pits of their wings.
The stained glass tremors
on the belly of the hump-back.

Jet

Her wrist had turned to dust:
become taste of must in the cave;
but her bracelet
slept through civilisations
sealed under stalagmite.
It is jet
and black as a calf's eye.

Up the Dale they call jet
candle-coal. They say,
'it's packed so tight
time can't get a finger in it.'

For Martin

Strange how gorse
has thorn and rich flower
both – all along
the hills and roadsides
from Carrowkeel to Portsalon
and on the slopes of Murren.

My Saviour caught his coat
on gorse. Fingering
the torn cloth and trammelled thread
he spoke of death being
thorn and rich flower,
both.

Midland Red

1

The tin sign tells us
they still sell Lion Tea
at the corner shop.
Gobstoppers
drop out for a penny
from full dispensers.
Stores sell back-studs
from miniature sets of drawers.
Everywhere, privet,
which short cuts to the ice-cream van
have rubbed bare.

2

Thanks to Littlewoods
a thousand Doreens
catch their fingernails
in their Mix 'n' Match
Nylon frilled pillow-cases.

In the Berni Inn Rogues Bar
we get curly butter,
and say,
'How about rosé?'

3

The pensioner with his pass
as creased as his trouser crotch
revolves his tea-stained dentures
and calls the driver, 'Driver!'

The colour of the washing
is mainly pink,
blown up like a wind-sock
over the dahlias.
Red and black for Ansells.
Fire and coal.
Lipstick and cinders.

Winston Churchill

On the morning of the funeral,
when the cranes were practising their salute,
the Myth woke up to his last responsibility.
He elbowed his way into his braces,
each shoulder some sort of clinched strategy,
and the trousers settled like theatre curtains
over the last generation of shiny shoes.

The responsibility lay around
our semi in the form of symbols
just a bit too big to manage:
the British Warm that gave me aircraft-carrier
shoulders; five inches of measly bath water;
and a rhetoric, which my father could turn on
for the small fee of being believed.

New College Dining Hall

The stampede went that way,
and it's sabbath again.
The benches breathe out,
while up there a ruff
goffered like a paper dart
in a rectangle of varnish
semaphores to the last Warden.
He is casual: legs crossed, grey suit,
hush-puppies. I sense that
eating is just a fraction
of the mute affair.
The rest is high old air:
spiralling, mote-filled.

Dusk at Lough Derryduff

The evening opened out like that.
We gradually put on silhouettes
like pullovers, and joined the march
of rushes, carrying their panicles

across the sky. Gumboots thudded the turf,
leaping the bog.
The parents way behind,
sounding as if along with us.

We got to the cars first,
and sat with the rods and the picnic case,
on the verge, willing the cloud
to cover the moon's bright face.

The keys came last.
The boot was stuffed. The dog, stowed.
We heaved each other's boots off;
saw liquid lights tremble in deep crofts.

Driving home, the simple line of hills
made finger-tracing
easy on the windows, still
thick with condensation from the dog's breathing.

Beeleigh Abbey

That particular prime
when the corncrake and the scent
of the goldflower met in the air,
the monks chose the Blackwater.
White habits worked the marsh: settled
like gulls on a burnt field.

But the monks are gone now,
and their prayer is aorist too.
Perhaps the tide stole it away
for salt: gathered it
on the sunken ribcage of the ferry.

The Seamen's Reading Room, Southwold

Cricket pavilions are like this:
photos crowding the walls; outdoor furniture
inside; the same uneven floor.
Instead of teams, here are skippers,
their oilskins fading from sepia to jaundice,
their pin-eyes daring the horizon.

Back at the clubhouse, one
stands up to deal, sits, fans his hand,
throws a casual card, with all his arthritis
moves a heavy match along.
He remembers when the tide was trumps,
or the gale; long before this foursome
became a model of itself.
The one in the corner fingers
his newspaper like a net.

The Book of Common Prayer 1549

This is just what you might expect
a Prayer Book to be like. This is
what we always thought about rain;
about dying, and marriage, and God.
We needed only the help which
the right placing of a relative pronoun
could manage. Words, then, said what they meant;
they bit. A man was a houseband
until death departed him.
And all was for common use:
printed in Fleet Street,
at the sign of the sun,
over against the conduit.

On Visiting Keats House

I had anticipated the wall-to-wall
carpet; the bookstall; and the staff toilet;
but not the brown ink of Keats' handwriting:
neat, round, and vertical.
Our duffle coats, when we leaned
on the glass to read this letter to Fanny,
gave a slight tap of toggle. We read,
with eyes only, a postscript full of dashes
and torment. I recalled the ring
he sent her, which she hid under a thin glove.
We replaced the cover, bought cards,
and left: aware that even one's frustration
from now, would be an imitation.
That if we were brave enough to say what we felt
this winter, it would have been said before,
in ink the colour of tea, to perfection.

Early Communion

Checking times the day before by brushing
blown snow off a leaning board, I guessed
that eight o'clock would chime
on a handful of us, and the priest.
The service was according to the book
the only variables being
my random fist of coins scooped into a bag
and the winter jasmine above the holy table.
For the rest, we knelt where it advised us to,
ungainly but meaning it, trusting to the words set
(on paper difficult to separate)
that what we did was acceptable.

After Mass

There is a way of setting down vestments:
chasuble, girdle, stole, alb;
and the amice, which is Christ's blindfold.
Each morning they come orderly off,
before the priest settles back into his belt
and considers breakfast.
A vague prayer at the altar rail
is nailed with the sign of the cross;
and as the trebles in the vestry
hit the sky with a practice scale,
he rises. The mass is done.
Another day is satisfied.

Heveningham Hall, Suffolk

Wandering through someone's planned
view between lake and mansion,
I excite lambs snaffling at dugs,
and lope through small acres of chancy sun.
This is spring and a stately home.
In a decade my half ticket
will be found in Crabbe's *Poems*,
and the *Illustrated Guide*
will be uncurled the other way.
Through one long corridor of rooms
I notice silk, shredding beneath
plastic sheets; and mirrors
shrinking in their gilt frames.
The relief of coming out is the door
encouraging the sun to make geometry
out of the stone floor.

Cycling Holiday

They prop up the tandem outside the shop,
exchange toffees, slot cards for the parents
into the wall. The wind is fresh
and tugs at the map where tanned fingers
trace the next stretch: lunch
safe in the panier. The shop bell
rings out a regular customer; and they are set
ready on the pedals. But just a moment
while he scratches his bare knee
and she rearranges her pony tail.

A Walk near Fulford Hospital

The wind tugging the couch-grass
and racing the Edinburgh express
across flat, soaked fields
stopped short at the hospital.

There I imagined patients fumbling awake
making mouldy heat out of yesterday's breath;
the sash windows painted into position.
The heat from the cream radiators
paled those who pressed against them;
and the cords, meant to puppet the ventilation,
had long since been pulled completely through.

Grateful for the freedom
to angle into the wind,
I noticed both the ridging on the elm
and the tangled raffia of potato stalks;
the cowl of my coat turning at will
as I walked, in and out of the ruts, home.

T.E. Lawrence to George Brough

It is the silkiest thing
I have ever ridden,
better than the Triumph in Cairo.
Yours has the spring sprocket
making it so mild at 50.
Stretching the goggles
over the shiny peak; gauntlets
flexed comfortably on, I move the two ends
of this long machine into a single bird
gathering speed through the open barrier
which drops its salute behind me.
We know the flat road into Cambridge;
the changes of gear around Ayot St Lawrence;
the midges on the Surrey switchback.
With my visor down so to speak I charge
at Mr Hardy's country to make it
back to camp before lights-out.
Thank you for the spare plugs.
I only needed one: the other
lasted till I got to Welwyn.
It is a perfect steed.

A Prayer at the putting on of our clothes

By our beds we were given a chair
and on it went the simple clothes of the day.
Each had the same sort
and all were grey.
This was what had to be, until four o'clock
and then 'scruff dress', softer at the edges,
meant baggier trousers, aertex shirt, pullover.
Grey was still the colour. We chanced nothing else
except for the tie which was maroon and dark blue.
Almost grey. This order had its effect.
Now the old changes of clothes are still around
to challenge the new. Why this? Why that?
Is it work or play today? Worse still
we go by the weather and change and change all day.
My prayer is again for the simple grey.

Old English Household Life
by Gertrude Jekyll, 1925

Nostalgia was just browning up
especially with regard to household things
in West Surrey when Gertrude Jekyll wrote.
Museums were typing out the labels
with a black typewriter's huge letters:
dog turnspit, smock, pepper pot.
Even then we were being removed from dirt
and the patient keeping in of lights and fires.
The brasses, no more catching the sun,
came off the sweating foreheads of the horses,
onto the pub wall. Lych-gates no longer
rested the dead on the final walk up the path.
Each chapter heading was an epitaph.

Rain

This is the rain the Brontës knew
knocking at the tomb-chests
like knuckle-bones thrown to dogs.
The drains drink to bursting.
The yews blacken, and the grass
toughens against the stones
ripening against the scythe.
The sisters have exercise books
from which they look up now and then
to watch the rain, in rods, refreshing
the dead, and memories of the dead.

Mist

It was always the same drawing;
a house on a hill
with a path winding to the door
and the sun beating down.
I saw a house the same today
just below the mist, and wondered
how another drawing could say
people live there now?
What could convey the placing of clocks?
Or the weight the seats take between bouts
of work? Or how the overalls
hoisted between hams
take a long time to dry
on days when the damp
gets even into the fire?
A brush stroke would do:
slanting the roof, rubbish by the path
too heavy to move, sheep's wool
hanging vertical from the wire.

Herdwick

Some work the sampler of the moor
their Quaker grey heads
following the text, stitch by stitch.
Others take a journey
at a tinker's pace, their wagon of rags
splashed with ochre, leadening in the rain.
The rest recline, passing the parcel
with their jaws, yet adamant
in their own seat, happy or not to win.

Flanking Sheep in Mosedale

All summer the sheep were strewn like crumbs
across the fell, until the bracken turned brittle
and it was time they were gathered
into the green patchwork of closer fields.
Dogs and men sweep a whole hillside in minutes
save for the stray, scared into a scramble
up a gully. A dog is detached: whistled off
by the shepherd who in one hand
holds a pup straining at the baling twine
and in the other, a crook light as a baton.
His call cuts the wind across the tarn:
it is the voice of the first man, who
booted it across this patch to bring
strays to the place where he would have them.
You can tell that here is neither love nor money
but the old game fathers have taught sons to win.
It is done well, when the dogs
lie panting, and the sheep encircled dare not move.

Curlew

The mist deadened the island
but the curlew swerving over the outhouse
was the last to succumb. Its bill
like a tool the sailmaker has to hand
is so turned as to glide in on the worm
in the sand; its cry, sharp as a blade on a strop.
In all this muffled dusk, little,
except a filling burn, and this bird,
beating the bounds of its woollen cage.

Border Ballad

Nothing untoward this morning
as the sun lifts the long-necked
hollyhock back up the garden wall;
and the snail's signature
silvers an unkempt path.
Only later the post arrives
with its heavy crested paper
folded in four, and the flimsy one
from the war. Then we can see
as the evening comes, and from this height,
all ten fingers of rain
press home their curse
into the steel water of the Firth.

Ruskin's *Sketches from Nature*

There is a hurry in his sketch. The cloud
will only stay a while like that
before a serious change obliterates.
A cloud will not stay quiet: it burns
and draws in all that is around,
cusping and reeling across the Old Man of Coniston.
On his desk are the practice wads
of cotton, and the books to verify
what a cloud is. He delights to find
that clouds do not grow, but are sculpted down
by the warm air around, like masons
working on Venetian stone. How difficult
to get them down on paper.
So many sacks of flour. Except for Turner
the master of the cloud, who in his vignettes
and storm studies seemed to get them right.

Quodlibet

It would be a good title.
It pleased Duns Scotus
and we share initials.
All those airy questions packed
into the neat hutch of a Latin word;
quodlibet: exactly separating this from that.
It got to such a pitch with him,
and I know how he felt,
that his stomach would not settle
for less than the essence of a thing.
The pleasure of getting it right
meant he could draw the blankets
round his chin, and sleep tight.
The converse I find is true,
tossing this way and that,
sorting out which, if any,
of the possible conditional clauses, will do.

William Nicolson
(1655-1727)

A boy from Plumbland
who took to declensions and tables
till the wax waterfalled and sputtered
has left us his notes
legible, on churches, churchyards,
wild flowers and rare words.

From the concern for detail
I had imagined a saintlier face.
The portrait, leaning out on long strings,
has it ruddy against lawn,
filling out with dinner towards the gilt frame:
one on the stairs at Rose, the other in the Hall at Queens.

He was a born Archdeacon, committed
to journeys and the minute particular;
and caustic, rowing with the Dean
over matters of protocol.
His pocket knife handy
for the constant scraping of lichen
from the thin lines of Norse runes.

Of the generation who wondered
on which day in March the Deluge commenced,
and the exact timing of the Fall;
their accuracy miscalculated God
but produced nice diagrams of the Roman Wall.

It mattered to him that the sanctuary was swept
and how the library at Derry was kept;
and for joy in the summer season, a dozen letters
or so, and rambling, simpling etc.

Dean Tait

*(Archibald Tait was Dean of Carlisle. In the space
of one month, March 1856, five of his daughters died
in an epidemic of scarlet fever.)*

Quite put aside were any thoughts
of the state of the Cathedral roof
Instead, a quiet agony, waiting
for the stethoscope's final figure of eight,
and the click of the doctor's bag.
He never thought there could be this routine
to death: the prayer book, the size of his palm;
his wife, half in doubt because of the fever,
hiding the sick-room drawings away;
and at their prayers each day
in a borrowed house, they tested
the Bible texts against a silent nursery.

David Livingstone on the eve
of discovering the Victoria Falls

The lamp picks out the flint-lock
a page of the Greek text of Luke,
his tin travelling-box, and his cap's red satin
upturned, holding open the notebook
at today's new words: *thunder, smoke,
waiting, rainbow.* On these nights of clear skies
he is grateful for his warm shirt,
its Scotch wool; at the end of the night,
this noise. The roar draws near.
The roar and the smoke have become familiar,
more thunderous: more like fire than water.
Another day will tell, another night,
what water burns, what fire ignites both rainbows.

Gwen John

Her cats move freely
about the room, while
dusk thins its colour
down to ash and
less takes over from more.
She has in mind a girl
whose hand rests in its lap
gentle from illness.
A Mother Superior
has the same stillness;
and villagers with comfy hats
settle into their seats in church.
She moves the quiet edges of the world
into line, and places a teapot within reach.

The Presbytery Cellar

It was like a potting shed
the warm sea-light falling on the suitcase,
the statues, the thurible hanging on the door knob:
all the brown junk that never made it
back to church. No housekeeper
would dare the steps under the electric wires
looped like bunting; only the priests
annually for the crib, or in search
of the patches and glue to mend a tyre,
went down cautious, smoking, out of breath.
After each half-jammed drawer, a puff,
a limp refusal to go on. What use
a rusty soutane button, a veil
yellowing to the colour of sherry.
Again there was no cause
to unpack the copies of the Fathers
sent from the Mother House.

The Burial of Mrs Pusey

The ruffle of crêpe and silk
moved round the quadrangle, shuffling
black and scarlet, faces alabaster
against the tidy, honey stone
into an unpredictable wind.
Gloved hands could hold veils down
but one thing lay beyond reach.
Doctor Pusey knew that well, but
it had not been so much brought home
as when the pall fluttered
like an uneven breath.
Something in the levity of it
locked for ever over that pavement
his melancholy tread.

Roof

The roof is for keeping out rain.
Good Welsh slate it is
set neat on the lath
overlapping the join beneath.
Not for drying flax this roof,
but angled to survive remarkable weather.
After each lashing I look
to see how the ranks have fared
and notice how they lighten
back in colour to the same purple-green.
There were days when the rain
went straight through, and the slates
got stacked in the long grass.
It was worth knocking it all out
and starting, from the shoulders of the wall, again.

Playing in the Yard

His hands seem to say
this toy is quite good
one large plastic ring through five,
colours shocking to the eye,
but it lies now where he threw it.

Ah yes, the gardening boot is better
fitting the whole of him,
a mysterious well
into which he drops his voice.

Better still, the pocket of the pram
feeling for tissues and old biscuits;
until the toy, neon in the grey yard,
flashes its frantic appeal.

Scale Model

I thought the view was familiar.
We made it one Summer Term just like that:
hills, patchwork fields, a river's meander;
and lead sheep permanently at grass.
It was a project for Open Day when we enforced
enclosure acts with a deft cut of foam rubber.
Peasants' cottages leant perilously up against themselves;
while the Manor stood solid in black and white gloss.
The model and the view collided, momentarily; but
the train sped on; and the mirror, which was a pond
slipped off the little world
turned up behind the stock cupboard.

Red Indian

One day, the tomahawk
split my brother's head.
He was General Custer,
and, as I thought, deserved it.
The blood made his hair shine black,
and in the quiet before the howl,
a breeze shivered the crows' feathers
down my bare, Red Indian back.

The Taste of Cast Iron

Some time before the Coronation
the playground was proposed
and seconded; the details
to be worked out later: like
who would pollard the limes
and grease the joints of the swings.
Since when the motor mower's throb
has ebbed and flowed all day
to the edge of the asphalt
and away to the putting green.
A thundery afternoon incubates
a mild nausea on the roundabout.
I can taste iron. From the top of the slide
there are all the roofs and gardens of the estate,
the coal bunkers, and bare patches on the lawn.
I taste the iron of fire-escapes and railings,
the bars of bus-stop barriers; gate latches;
and wash them down with one
slide after another.

Botanical Gardens

I was settled in this Eden
when he waved from a long way off
indicating it was closing time.
In slow motion I waved consent
and sauntered to the gate
over light shale, between precise edges of grass.
The Latin names came lazily off their signs:
take it or leave it; we are known.
Hoe blades now resting on the soil
shone with use. I slowed right down
for beyond the gate something disturbed the air
more than here: things with no name
or the wrong name; weeds; mud
drying on the spades. There seemed
no carrying out the secret of the place.
It snaked back, like the pipes
in the Glass House, to a hidden tap.

The Oxford Dictionary of Nursery Rhymes

These we let out,
like butterflies from spring window-sills.
They have slept a long time
but rise up from the memory
as we rock from foot to foot,
humming at first, then
our own version of the words,
See-saw, Margery Daw.

We like it in the barn
the beamed roof, the earth floor,
the sun angling through the doorway,
saying nothing, making logs
drop off the sawing horse
as if we had all day,
content with but a penny.

For Brother Jonathan

(Brother Jonathan, the guardian of Alnmouth Friary,
died after being washed out to sea on 31 July 1982.)

I remember the water. For a second
let it right over me.
It knocked out my breath
on the first eager morning there
before breakfast. All day
the waves breathed on to the sand and the sea–coal;
and at night, looking from the library
I think a beacon swept them
about the turn of every page.

The quiet and the sea: I thought
this was the life. It wasn't
entirely. You let me into that secret,
Jonathan, gently, and over the years
through the contents of a whole bundle
of brown envelopes said as much.

We met again in Cambridge, at the top
of a narrow staircase. You enjoyed
being contemporary with Charles.
That was part of you, as much
as the backache in the novitiate.

There were so many at the Profession
it was a matter of nods over heads,
and watching the damp rise up the servers' albs
on that wet day, under canvas, in the courtyard.
The blackberry picking and red polishing stone floors
were becoming things of the past.

We last met on the train going north.
It was hot and crowded;
you, in the unseasonal thick habit.
It was unsatisfactory again:

a matter of small talk, and I wondered
if it was the same for others,
where the knowing you well
was always yet to come.

Then the news in fragments:
your recent concern for fitness;
the shoes on the empty beach;
and day by day the certain possibility
of your being entirely out of reach.

The Orchard

Now we have apple trees
and a walled garden beyond the village.
Boys will come for the meagre, sour fruit
by way of the frames and the water butt.
It will be the heat of the day
they remember, when as old men
they make their mild confession
to the new incumbent. They will remember
the stalking through the undergrowth,
and the first sweat of guilt,
sweeter than the apple.
Eased out of a narrow pocket
it was worth only one tart bite
before an aimless chuck sent the birds
flying, and there was time to attend
to a graze and a pumping heart.

A Talk on William Byrd

The gas is turned on, but the old, soft
box of matches is not striking well enough.
The smell seeps through the iron shutters
from the kitchen into the Hall, thickening the air.
The few chairs for the talk on William Byrd
straddle the lines of the badminton court.
We face the back of the piano, beneath
a light bulb hanging like a plumb-line.
'This is the Ave Verum Corpus,' and the needle
is lowered into the second bar. Gas becomes incense.
Seagulls, like angels, glide through the aerials.

Bishop Taylor's Remedies Against
Tediousness of Spirit

I know the clergy around Llanfihangel
are sometimes out of sorts with the full
Morning and Evening Prayer, said each day.
My suggestion is that they sing
even alone in the church, what they always say.
It doesn't have to be Purcell
or Pelham Humphryes; anything
that touches the fancy will sound well
and return a relish to praying.

Parish Visit

Going about something quite different,
begging quiet entrance
with nothing in my bag, I land
on the other side of the red painted step
hoping things will take effect.
The space in the house is ten months old
and time has not yet filled it up,
nor is the headstone carved.
He died when he was twenty
and she was practised at drawing
him back from the brink
cajoling in spoons of soup.
We make little runs at understanding
as the winter afternoon
lights up the clothes on the rack;
we make so many
the glow in the grate almost
dips below the horizon,
but does not quite go out.
It is a timely hint
and I make for the door and the dark yard,
warmed by the tea,
talking about things quite different.

Scattering Ashes

The nose of the pick-up lifted
into the sky and then down onto the fell
as we made our way to the spot
he drove to himself to drop hay
in bad winters and as he got lame.
From where we stopped, we could see
the farmhouse and the tops of hills
which for a moment seemed to pour in
on the random heap of an old sheep pen.
Willy fed the ash out like a trail
of gunpowder. It blew among us
taking the words with it: ashes; sacred;
our brother here departed. We stood
fixed awkwardly as hawthorn trees watching
the white ashes of a man who once stamped
this ground, fly off in fancy with the wind.
Arms were wrapped like scarves round shoulders;
and the dog, whistled out of the back,
wove in front of the car a sad reel
as we followed the fresh tracks home
through all the open gates on the land.

from

PLAYING FOR ENGLAND

(1989)

Flower Rota

This is my week for flowers.
It half says so on the damp notice in the porch.
(I had to borrow the pen from the Visitors' Book
and the ink ran out before my name.)
A few, who have let fall into their hearts
similar tragedies to mine, know why I chose this week
when flowers are hard to come by.
Each year I tell the season by a bowl of flowers,
whether things are late or soon, and predict
with those who visit here while I arrange,
the future course of summer.
They don't know for whom I struggle
to get this stalk through the chicken-wire,
and it doesn't matter. When they are gone,
names half written in the Visitors' Book,
I'll have a moment when it's just
the flowers, the memory, and the sweet time it took.

Cross Canonby

The waves of the rigged field
beat against the ploughed sea.

Farmers and sailors: their headstones
akimber from persistent wind.

Rush light in the window, family Bible,
pend the docking of the clipper.

Tea, tobacco, turnips: the same face but
different boots share the year's saga.

Skiddaw House

The House was one of the loneliest
dwelling-places in all the British Isles.
HUGH WALPOLE

Left for us to assume what purpose
it once had other than shelter;
remote in the bowl of hills behind Skiddaw
deep in its own decay; the peace stuns,
the filth accumulates, the questions gnaw.
How did anyone manage? Did they feed
on the shifting view of mountain tops?
Why put the windows facing north-east?
Some say it was for the shoot,
for nights away from the Big House
to be near the butts. Others that
it was given to shepherds
for weeks at a time, and they survived
because they knew there was somewhere else
nearer the auction and the ale.
Yet what if once it had been a family
living there, taking silver water from the beck
and setting off for a day's walk
to Keswick or Bassenthwaite.
Growing up taught by the hills' silence;
reading the shifting mist; working out God's pattern
from this piece of it. The larch coppice
smoothed into shape by the wind.
The gate into the four rows of vegetables
now on one hinge.

Castlerigg Songs

I

Before dawn,
before chanting broke the wind's silence,
before shadows,
before the sheep's first tug at the grass
when the backs of the great beasts
resurrected in the light
there was the mystery.

II

Cleft fast in the stone's skin
is a lichen tuft. It is the air's
embroidery: silent, slow, patient, deft.

III

I throw up grass to see
which way the wind blows.
It is tugged all ways:
no shelter in any angle of the stones:
buttercup frantic in the wind:
wool holding tight to a blade of grass.

IV

There is to be one stone mightier than the rest:
a king of stones, from which all the land
can be seen and divided. This is the place.
Set it down here. Set others round it.
Make an order of stones
starting from the mighty stone.
Set it down for good.

v

No mark, no runes,
only the sheep's rubbing;
no illumination;
no face no feature;
I mark a place
that is all.
I set against fuss
stone, air, earth,
being born, death.

Playing for England

(for Robert Hanvey)

He sat by the boot shop window
fettling the studs for Saturday's match,
his apron slashed almost to shreds.
As farm carts bounced back from the fields
he thought of the new schoolteacher,
and the match. The Match.
It kept coming back to that.

The lasts, the knife, and the needle
were set aside for the weekend
so he could scrummage with unaccustomed
other shoulders. He left the last shoe
to be mended, with the thread dangling.

Chosen to play for England
in the year of the General Strike
he shook the hand of George V
at Twickenham. His white strip engaging
the king's black overcoat and bowler.

Rose on the chest, buttons and collar;
full, pocketed shorts; bandage garters;
dubbin and embrocation.
The rest was himself:
solid, neckless Cumberland.

The match was the usual mixture
of dread and exultation, cracking of heads,
snotting out of one nostril.
He gum-shielded his half-time orange
and on his hunkers took in the tactics.
The scrum steamed as the light dwindled.

Feeding out the notched leather strap
for letting the window down of the last train
he was the only one to alight:
tasselled, velvet cap in the bag.

London was a single bird's song away.

They lost, but never mind.
There was the home ground
looking up to the mountains;
the schoolteacher encouraging
her African violets; and round about
the folks' shoes to make and mend.

A Line of Wordsworth's

(after Théophile Gautier)

Of all the Wordsworth I have read (the poet
On whom Byron expended so much venom),
The only line I have by heart is
'Spires whose silent finger points to heaven.'

I found it as an epigraph
To the first chapter of *Louisa*,
A Virgin's Lament, in a book of short stories
Called *The Dead Donkey* – if you please!

This line, fresh and holy, dropped
Into a volume of sweaty affairs, moved me
As if it were a wild flower, or a bird's feather
Floating into a dark cellar.

Since then, when words will not be summoned –
My Prospero disobeyed by Ariel –
On the blank sheet of paper I doodle spires,
their silent fingers pointing to heaven.

Skiddaw

A headscarf tied beneath her jaw,
the curtains of her eyes drawn
and drawn back, we talked about Skiddaw.
How from childhood she watched the dawn
rise behind it, and now propped on pillows
she could see it darken against the night.
Always it had been there and would be always
long after our eyes were tight shut.
Perhaps it is enough for one life,
one mountain. Given time
she would have photographed it
in all weathers: sheeting down, fine.
It was to do with time and eternity
like Hokusai's passion for Mount Fuji,
and his saying, 'If heaven had given me
five years more, I should have been a great painter.'

Stones on a Dorset Beach

Stirring invisible dust, bleached
through millennia, we crunch our way
across a *Shell Guide to Dorset* beach,
picking up stones. I choose this one,
Adam that one. He says his,
a piece of cloudy glass the shape of a heart
and two pure white stones
suitable for a sling or a still life
are not as good as mine.
Mine are door stops. Lucy's
are the rare mottled brown ones;
and for Jonathan there is a rule:
'only as many as you can carry'.
Surveyed by the fossil-locked cliff
our bent heads and occasional stoops
signal both the random and the fixed.
The cove-long waves repeat their off rhythm.
Dust whitens our shoes.

Monday

Washing the regimental off-white woollens
by the crab apple tree, they smelt the malt,
flicked a glance at embedded bottles,
imagined their hair floating like the weed.
Lathering was hard, then the bashing
on the stones; wring, wrench; unravel;
wring, wrench; and a moment's pang
for the skin beneath the scarlet.
Unaware that the cholera rilled
along the stream; under their reddening knuckles
it filled the buckets all the way to the mill.

A Prayer on the North Side

The mowers can't get easily
over established tufts.

So the brambles tie up the parcels
of this ramshackle park.

While everyone files out of the south
I go to the north side to be soothed

by its lack of attention. The tall
unclipped yews wave a high hello.

Reading Party

Someone had a house by Windermere.
It was good air for a reading party.
So up they came: soft leather bags
containing delicacies, pushed down
between the clerical socks and the Tracts,
to compensate for the local fare.
In the earnest silence of the night
they surprised each other on the stairs,
and in the library searched for something
the fresh air did not seem to give them.
The mountains were not enough. They were
homesick for a Comper baldachino
to narrow down the glory. It took a week
for them to assume a doctrine of creation;
longer still to skim a pebble on the lake.

Locking the Church

It takes two hands to turn the key
of the church door, and on its stiffest days
needs a piece of iron to work it like a capstan.
I know the key's weight in the hand
the day begins and ends with it.
Tonight the sky is wide open
and locking the church is a walk
between the yews and a field of stars.
The moon is the one I have known
on those first nights away from home.
It dodges behind the bellcote
and then appears as punched putty or a coin.
The key has a nail for the night
behind the snecked front door.
Carrying a tray of waters up to bed
I halt a careful tread to squint
through curtains not quite met
at the church, the moon, and the silver light
cast on the upturned breasts of the parish dead
locked out for the night.

Excerpts from the Passion

(translations of George Herbert's Latin poems)

1 *On the Sweating*

Where do you run to, sweat?
Christ does not know, nor his veins.
Does it not please you to stay in that
body of all bodies? If not,
no other body will please you, I can vouch for that;
unless it's mine you're after,
the least worthy, to make you most worthy,
by my rescue.

2 *On the Spitting and Railing*

Savages, on the holy face, right side
which to look on is to live
you spit; and on the turned side
as fresh as the water of life, you spit
and swear. Beware
lest the whole fig tree race, right cheek
left cheek, be cursed. Good people of the living water
prepare cups, flagons, buckets,
the Aqueduct is yours.

3 *On the Buffeting*

My mother made a poultice
for chest colds; bashed it into a bread shape
with the heel of her hands.
So, remedy for all mankind
thou was spun round blind,
and beaten before, on top, behind.

4 *On the Whipping*

Christ, hope of the whipped, victor of the world
when crimes multiply, and my punishment draws near
may your more gentle whip, the shadow of your whip, suffice.
Tender minds duplicate blows for themselves.
Soft hearts are their own whips.

5 *On the Nails*

What sort wast thou
but a better nature
that took a less from ours
and was nailed to the cross.
Now thou art mine. I have thee.
The shepherd caught by the
nails and wood as if by his own scythe.

Churchyard under Snow

The newer headstones tense against the cold
having no moss to befriend the snow;
and footsteps to them are specific, directed
not for idle search, but to a particular bolster of earth.
Year long widowers right a tipped vase
and shake the Christmas wreath back into greenness.
A thrush cascades snow off a bouncing
high branch and offers its clear song
over the uniform white ground.
The cold makes it so much worse,
indiscriminate in its disregard
for the memory of this one's summer dress
and the angle of that one's cap over his shrewd brow.
We used to hurry them inside from the cutting wind:
now, from that unimaginable weathering
we can only trust their souls do well to fly.

The Surplice

To think so many battles have been fought
over this four and a half yard circumference
of white linen. Not just by those who ironed it
up to the difficult tucks beneath the yoke
but by Divines wrangling over rubrics.
For me it is my only finery, by law
decent and comely; a vestry friend
put on often in dread; given away
to old deft fingers to mend.
I have seen them hanging in as many ways
as there have been voices chanting in them:
immaculate in hanging wardrobes; or worn
with the peg mark still obtruding;

or chucked on the back seat of the car
with the purple stole and the shopping.
We have put these garments on for centuries.
They persist. We wither and crease inside them.

A Walk with St Teresa of Avila

We chose the low cliffs first, and then
to come back along the beach into the falling sun.
It was November and there was no wind, just
a bluish, evening mist.
She spoke of arrows wounding her heart, and stripping
everything away that came between her and Christ.
The breakwaters were bleached and purified
by a century of salt pounding tide.
The sun, a huge and softened red, reigned
above dark roofs and the steeple
as the lights came on beneath.
I think she didn't notice it was the eighteenth green
we finished up on; some late players were judging
the camber and then missing. In the clubhouse
by the light of table lamps, I saw the ladies
sorting cards out on the baize. Charitably,
Saint Teresa said that everyone is a bunch
of dried rosemary, and I could see the longing in her eyes
for more of the wounds of love and for the darts
that score the heart.

Hopkins Enters the Roman Catholic Church

Dressed mainly in black and with hair
shading the upper lip,
he took the railway from Oxford
to Birmingham; fingernails, collar, notebook
all much grubbier than we would suppose.
The journey was an absolute offering
in the dark. The tunnels confirmed this.
The shattering thunder of iron
recalled the opposition to his choice:
Father, Mother, Canon Liddon –
'Do have the courage to stop, even now.'
In his notebook, the design
for a decanter stopper. Looking at the oaks
in the parks he wondered how he would get
to the Oratory on the Hagley Road.
For comfort he thought that being alone
might double charge his spirit, but good,
they were expecting him, and yes,
he was Mr Hopkins and this was
all he had brought. They arrived in the dark,
and the leaves blown into the hall of the house
scratched on the chequered floor
as far as Doctor Newman's room.

Atkinson of Danby

It seemed essential for him to stay put
resisting all offers of preferment
or a move nearer the shops at Scarborough.
He found it difficult at first, missing
the softness of the Essex marshes,
and coping with a sour and empty church;
but as the Lents and Trinitys came round
for the fortieth time, he no longer searched
for novelty beyond the parish bounds.
It was largely the Yorkshire turn of phrase
that held him tightly to his moorland place
listening, writing it down for the Glossary.
He dug words out, like earth chucked
shoulder high from a deepening grave.
The shards and bones of the old talk,
as well as a few faithful souls, were saved.

Richard Watson Dixon

(1833-1900)

Left-handed you wrote into your ink
incorporating references
to tenth-century monks
and the British garden birds.
Scanning the long poems
for anything left behind by the critics
I was hoping for a gem
fired in the rectory in the room
overlooking the tennis court.
I sometimes wonder if the poems
had been more a matter of life or death
rather than an adjunct to
your *History of the Church of England*
there might have been a masterpiece
with lines that soldiers called to mind
and girls took through to lonely womanhood.
Hubris was your talent,
and sadness,
and putting poems, it seems,
where they are hard
but not impossible
to find.

Village Organist

1 *Short Prelude*

Grace was sung to Melcombe
(New Every Morning is the Love)
while the polish and turnips
mulched to an indelible memory
for the pianist. She was ten.
Her legs dangled above the pedals.
It was the vicar's wife took notice
knowing that Melcombe would do
for almost any hymn, and asked
if Mary Ann could be encouraged
to play a hymn in church.
There were always boys to blow the organ
but rarely girls to play it.
So this was a discovery
unheard of from the village.

2 *Introductory Voluntary*

The vicar led her to the organ
as if to some returning aunt
she had never met before. It stood there
straight-backed with its decorated pipes,
ivory keys, and knobs –
'Oh! the stops, don't worry about those
just pull them all out' –
the high up importance of the seat
with its piece of Turkey carpet cushion.

'Try Melcombe,' said the vicar, 'I'll pump for you
this once.' The pumping was vigorous,
distracting, his white shirt
flapping from behind his stock.
In two sharps were blown
the first few notes of a lifetime's playing.

From then on, the weekly list of hymns
would come before her, numbers
as resonant as the words. With each new vicar
she gauged the announcement of the hymn:
some brisk, some devotional, some didactic;
as various as the boys who came
to pump for her, the vicar's lads
who, when the blower went electric,
slipped away onto the tractor seats
careless of Sunday.

3 *Funeral March*

> '*It was proposed that the organist be given £2*
> *a year advance in salary – on the understanding*
> *that she would play at funerals when desired.*'

She would play them in and play them out
and for bride as well as coffin
she would squint through her curtain screen
hat bobbing back and forth
to catch the vicar's sign or his voice
'I am the resurrection and the life...'
Between The Lord's My Shepherd
and Abide With Me she browsed among
the clothy pages of her annotated hymn book:
the vicar's favourite; verses to omit
from the long processional hymns;
alternative tunes borrowed from the chapel.
Her shoe heels safe
behind the cross-bar of the stool.

4 *Second Tune*

*'The organist of a parish church, although appointed
and paid by the vestry, is guilty of an ecclesiastical
offence if he plays on the organ during Divine service
contrary to the directions of the incumbent.'*

Not long before she retired for the first time,
there was the terrible day of the note. That week
the vicar decided on the second tune
for a familiar hymn. The choirmistress was informed
but she did not like it. The practices were hard work.
The second tune did not flow like the first one.

Come the day of the first time to sing the new tune,
right in the middle of the service, a note came
from the choirmistress to the organist –
'Play the old tune.'
The organist went cold. The open diapason bass
thrummed all through her, gonging
in her empty stomach. She loved the vicar.
She was terrified of the choirmistress.

The hymn was announced,
and she would always remember this,
she would date her life before and after it,
she played the new tune. Why should pain
like this get even into the chancel?

The vestry was somewhere she never went,
but this day, the day of the terrible note,
she went into its strange, curtained
unfamiliarity and cried, caught between two wills.
The vicar, versed in law and handkerchiefs,
helped her to wipe the tears, and later,
to face the choirmistress from whom
because of the distance to the branch-line
there was no immediate escape.

5 *Chanting the Proper Psalms*

The Cathedral Psalter had such a dark cover
that she often mislaid it in the gloom.
The word 'cathedral' gave her aspirations
which she transposed for the meagre congregation:
two of whom were deaf; one always without her glasses;
and the one who found the twenty third morning
in time to catch the 'Glory be to the Father'.
The words in her book took on a new intensity
with their upright strokes marking off
the syllables, and there were asterisks
which, coming at the end of a long line
when they could sing no more without exploding,
allowed them breath. What the references
to Leviathan or the water-pipes meant
was another matter. Winter's meaning
seeped into summer's stone; meaning
was there when they needed it,
brought on by the repetition of the days.

6 *Finale*

In the end it got too much for her, as one finger
after another went permanently cream.
She was waking at four to play at nine.
In her mind her last service would have been the finest
with all her favourite tunes; instead,
it was a new invention for Christmas
with songs the children were meant to know
with the words stuck up on the walls.
The icy wind seemed against her both ways
as she went to get her pension. Church
was the last straw. After the service
as her bandaged ankle passed the garage
they suggested she came in and sat down.
It seemed there were no tunes left in her,
and to all who stopped for petrol, it was declared
that she was ill, and the unspoken verdict was

that, as far as the organ was concerned, that was it.
As for the hymn books and music, well,
they could stay where they were
with the notebook, her glasses, and her pencil.

Brother Douglas Looks After the Bees

The hives were somewhere near the apple trees,
(the Standard W. Broughton Carr Hive)
white, with room for the bees to live,
room to expand, and room to thrive.
He would set off with three essentials:
cat, garden fork, boater with veil,
looking like something from the Army and Navy Stores
by way of Lady Ottoline Morrell.
The way to the bees was through central Italy.
Dorset was Umbria: the one burnt, with ilex trees,
the other lush after it had poured;
one with ox and cart, the other with a worn-out Ford.
When the sun of the canticle did not shine
he did his best with the whitewash,
the naming of the houses (Juniper, Clare), Mowbrays'
reproductions, and costumes for the Housman plays.
His gloveless manipulation of the bees
satisfied an instinct in him which was Franciscan,
energy controlled by stillness,
England and Italy combining
in the laughter and the ceaseless gardening.
It was a problem of language too.
Italian vowels reduced to the tight precision
of a Saxon consonant: from Giacomo to James
a pulling in of the reins; from *sole* to sun
to do with the magic of just catching it.
On the morning of the photograph
the sun caught one lens of his spectacles;
the hives; and later in the day
escaped between beeches all the way to Dorchester Market,
onto jars of honey clanking in the back.

The Sunday School Cupboard

It has all become unusable,
another generation's way of doing things,
and yet there is no throwing it out.
I would save them from others' dustbins:
the wall pictures wrapped in a great bundle
unrolled reveal the angels ascending
and descending on a crumpled ladder.
The felt-backed shepherds and the stamp books
with rusty staples should have gone long ago.
All of Advent Sunday's stamps
are stuck together in a great wodge.
A book for the teacher written for
two hundred children who could sit still.
The vital pegs for the blackboard,
the light wooden cross, the wrapover hymns,
the prayer cards passe-partouted,
the cigar-box carpenter's bench,
which has its shavings still inside
breathing a devotion to the geography
of the Holy Land, recall the ghosts of spinsters
devoted to the rector. While the parents
slept off their week's work and Sunday lunch
this teacher made her register a work of art
and for the children caused the heat to shimmer
over the road from Jerusalem to Jericho.

The Marquis of Ripon Purchases
the Convent of San Damiano

Up a steep hill and out of town,
looked after by a shuffling, aproned verger
doubling as housekeeper to the priest
was Ripon's Roman Catholic Church,
St Wilfred's; where Lord Ripon lit the first
eager candles of his conversion.
Was it there the idea came to him
to buy back San Damiano's from the State,
at a time when places such as those
were realising very low prices?
He thought of all the place had meant to him
(cicadas, cypress, thyme,
the ancient conjunction of wood and stone,
the lack of any compulsion to respond)
when he had visited there with his friend
and water-colourist, W.B. Richmond.
The Count of Cavour would have knocked it down,
used the benches for levering gun-carriages
out of the mud in his fight against the Austrians,
and stolen the brittle, silver hair,
probably not St Clare's, and used it
for stuffing King Victor Emmanuel's footstool.
But there, Francis heard the crucifix speak,
and Clare wrote letters to the Blessed Agnes of Prague
signing herself 'useless handmaid'.
For these and other reasons, Lord Ripon paid
all those noughts of lires
arguing over the exchange of currency
and mistranslations, so that the nuns
could filter back under no pressure to be useful.
San Damiano's, the place where Francis wrote
Il Cantico di Frate Sole, under its Yorkshire landlord
was returned to an acre of grace.

The Closure of the Cold Research Institute

Was it at Berkhamsted or Tring?
Well, anyway, it's just packed in.
Boffins' heads like Friedrich Nietzsche's
are seen emerging from the Chiltern beeches.
Olitsky and Macartney with files untold
have failed to trap the common cold.
We've got the hang of the other species,
we can tell which are the foreign cheeses.
Most common things we understand:
sparrows, cormorants, Prayers, and land,
but colds defy the common wit.
You get them, and that's it.
So that's it too for volunteers
and bottles labelled over many years;
tons of bumph and Government Issue
pulped into rolls of lime green tissue.
Still the nation's noses run
impervious to tots of rum.
The mother's eagerness to wipe
is countered by the child's swipe.
The dreadful sweat of boardroom meetings,
the midnight shakes, the fitful sleeping,
days off school, off work, off life,
the 'don't come near me's' of the wife,
all these presumes a fierce defiance
of man's experimental science.
We cannot check the flow of phlegm
or staunch the faulting speaker's 'hem'.
So if there are no more suggestions,
we'll have to be content with questions:
Which of the primates had it first?
Which of the Royal's had it worst?
If God intended it for man
what exactly was his plan?

The Church Boiler

Robert W. Pitt Ltd. Milburn House (B Floor), Newcastle-on-Tyne.
For one new six Section Water Circulating Boiler supplied
and fitted in position to your satisfaction. Removing
old Boiler and connecting up to your existing pipes as
arranged ---------------------------------*£41-10*
26th November, 1932

1st August, 1932

Dear Mr Pitt, I'm told
it's possible you have a better system
of heating to offer to a poor parish
than the old one we have, which is furred up
and has poor circulation, so that some radiators
are starved of heat. The complaints
are justified. Something must be done,
of course it must, and it is my
responsibility: not only preaching sermons
but also keeping the people warm.

10th September, 1932

I'm so pleased that you can help. Newcastle
seems a long way from Cumberland:
you and your man will spend the night, I hope,
and over here we have a man who helps.
We are so dependent on the goodwill
of the sexton. He does his best:
coming every Saturday night with his torch,
he shovels the coke, lights the boiler,
and carts away the ash. I can hear it
from the Vicarage but leave him to it
hoping he keeps a straight path to the ash-pit.
He will do anything for you except come to church.

15th September, 1932

You say the new boiler will be larger
and displace the coke. That will mean a new
coke pile and a lean-to for it. More work for the sexton;
more requests for kindness. How difficult I find that!
Bob will do it, but his pace
will signify that it's a favour. I'd do it myself
but then he'd say it was his job.

12th October, 1932

I don't understand the significance
of an increase of 20,000 Thermal Units.
All I know is what a difference it makes
to be warm, and how it will cost
more than we can think of or can easily manage to pay.
But this must be the story everywhere,
and a Sale will go a long way to meet the cost.
So whenever you and your man can come
we shall be pleased to see you. I'll ask the sexton
if he can help, when he's not busy at the Garage.

7th November, 1932

When you left last Monday
and we thought everything was fine
one of the small pipes on the boiler
had commenced to leak. There's always
something, isn't there. Could you get a new fitting
sent through with your man?
We would like to light up the boiler for the service
on the Twenty Third Sunday after Trinity.
For the last few Sundays
it's been cold here, but not severe.
How dependent we are in our Church for warmth.
We cater largely for the old.

23rd November, 1932

I'm sorry to trouble you again
but the boiler now seems to be overheating.
I know you'll understand if I say that a service
held under threat of an explosion is not conducive
to the rest and quietness advocated by the Evening Collect.
It makes everyone nervous. The sexton
says that it's probably easy to control
but he would value your opinion.

13th December, 1932

We have taken note of your suggestion
and installed, at least the sexton has,
a pipe which can take the overflow of boiling water.
That is a relief. Such a simple thing
needing just 'a little common reason' as you say.
We have put a thermometer by the lectern
so every time I read the lesson I think
of your common reason and the fount
of heavenly wisdom. The Sale helped raise the funds,
and we have pleasure in settling your account.

Whit Monday

We parked between what was left of the great forest
and the area set aside for the sheepdog trials,
where Elliots and Frasers in battered suits
whistled their dogs into the utmost stealth.
Morris men, arms and legs going both ways,
trod the deep vat of courtyard chippings
while the Regimental Band puffed among the topiary
waiting for the capering with handkerchiefs to end.
The Dean popped up now and then from counting the cars.
It was far too cold to lounge about, and some,
still shaky from a dose of winter 'flu
edged their way through the vintage cars
to their own securer model with its rug and tissues.
A helicopter growled at the retreating, long grass.
The voice from the by-election speakers was a help
but the wind blew it out of range
as one hand struggled with the cornets
and the other fished under the plastic mac for change.
Trodden grass gave off its own smell.
We were about the last to leave. The emptying park
revealed the bales of straw by the marquee.
The car was lighter by a picnic; heavier
by a garden plant, bought just to show we'd been.
We took a fresh grass route out: the so-called grown-ups
in the front, and strapped into the back,
the emperor and empress of ice cream.

Maths Master

Cambridge was his only real time away
when the Senior wranglership gave vent
to his one brief exclamation of joy.
At other times it was shy, pointed comments
humphed out of an anxiety to keep all angles
perfect. On the full-sized billiard-table it went
white to red, red off the cushion, and red pocketed;
upstairs the gramophone speakers and chair arranged
for the maximum stereo effect; and on holiday
climbing Scafell or Snowdon, unencumbered,
he strove to make the route isosceles.
Boyhood, manhood, old age spent
in the same school, round the same paths.
Theorems, chalk, marks: a celibate for Maths.
Any deviation from the rule he could not bear.
When errors occurred that ought not to have done
in his own handling of things, like adding up,
he slipped by night and without a word
to anyone, into Archimedes', by then cold water.

For Norman Nicholson

It was a long way round from
Ulverston on the road to Millom.
We passed the low sands and the gulls
and the first outcrop of the hills
until at 'the west of the west'
– his phrase – we reached a film set
of the 1930s, stage and props.
You could tread on a whole row of shops
and chapels. So many corners to lean against.
So much shoring up of the corrugated fence.
That must be the house
with its old shop window doused,
where you can sit in the back
and join in the front street crack.
Over the roofs, Black Combe,
and yonder the silent doom
of Windscale. All this has been set
down in words, from the Good Friday sonnet
of the first wartime anthology
to the dazzle of the Easter Sunday sea.

Childhood Triptych

I

Stammering his way out of
the priesthood,
perpetual deacon
never at the altar
more under the black cloth
left hand waving out messages
to stay still
stay still, my little girl,
'that's beautiful'.

II

So black at one moment
except for the wide eyes
beneath the cap
above the knotted scarf
saying 'why, o why'.
And then all white
and wings and fronds
of drifting weed in the river
swimming naked over the black deep.

III

Some inevitable confusion
between the window wide open
to the night and the curtains blowing
and the sail on my boat
flapping, adrift on the pond.
Between a boy and a girl
looking out in wonder
at a painted sky, and
wondering myself how grandma
could be so foolish as to let go
the string as she launched my boat.
So that when I see the one
I see the other, and when I see the other
I see the one: park and play,
statue and lost boat.

Just a line

(for Geoffrey Holloway)

It happened
having just cracked the spine
that my eye
and mind found the perfect
converting line.
Before was never
the same as after.
The line will go with me
to the grave, perhaps
see me through it.

It was something to do with
a swimming pool
and the feeling of trust
between swimmer
and water, father
and daughter.

I had felt it
and you had said it,

poet.

Packers

When it was Mr Lawrence
and Mr Hall, in the days
of tea chests and dust sheets,
and labels tied with coarse, hair string
you just had to ask and they would know
which hold and for how long.
After all, these suits
flat arms folded in and letters bundled
and the stones and the driftwood
packed within the packing
were part of you, were you.
They were things that you would miss.

Mr Lawrence and Mr Hall
appreciated this.

Hamada

O for just the deft
touch of a Hamada
in my teaching –
bold, thick strokes
fearless of mistake.
He used to walk along
a line of pots, a pupil
holding the paint,
asperging them.
Nothing could go wrong.
With every pot he hit the mark.
The merest flick: a song.

Daffodils

In winter when I pass that orchard
I forget what it can be like. Dashing
to the library, dentist, or garage
there seems no time to remember.
The orchard is just over a hedge, and has four
or five apple trees: a place to peg out washing,
let chickens roam, tie a swing. Pleasing
but not enough to stop me in my tracks.
My neighbour who cycles that way every day
will know what I mean when I say,
April is different. All winter
clenched in frost or sogged in rain
they hide. Today I stop the car,
no errand too important for honouring,
with some awkward parking, the sight in sun and wind
of this green and yellow jamboree of daffodils.

Pulling Out Weeds

Whoever hath a mind to weed will never want work.

Buttercup

It accepts a firm grip at the waist
and a shake of its skirt of root
to free it from the loosened soil.
It comes without complaining, hands up.
Its languishing butter heads
slopping out of the wheelbarrow.

Forget-me-not

At the end of May,
from this skirt of washed blue
under the apple trees
as much as on a market day
we'll take a few, making an alleyway
for boots and bare knees.

Ground Elder

Preferring shale and bits of glass
to bed in and flourish, linked
in a mafia of underground handshakes,
only gentle handling will reveal the connections
and then it will come out whole
like a lifted jigsaw.

Dandelion

Leave them as a field of brittle haloes
until the last second blows away
and then dig deep for its carrot root.
The root is tough as the stalk is brittle.
To crack the naked hollow stalk in idler days
meant a slippery rub and the bitterest spittle.

Daisy

The soil's brooch. It will come off
from behind, by teasing its clasping thin roots
away from the mud; but used to a tight lawn
it will not always come clean.

Cow Parsley

You can tell by the crown of lace and the tall walk
that this is her wedding day.
It takes two hands in a tug-of-war
to lift her from her primacy.
She knows where her strength lies
and she is holding on to it.

Nettle

Some can take them by the hand, the old gardeners.
Others pick them for their goodness.
I tackle them low
where their ragged turkey necks of stalk
have no leaves, no chance of mottling the skin,
no need for spit and docks.

The Wild Boar

(the wild boar was the emblem of the Twentieth Legion)

The scratchable hide crashing the bracken,
snuffling for roots in the vile weather,
racing from the spear. This was the beast
it was the legionary's duty to carve
on his section of the wall. A cognisance.
He imagined the turning spit, the singeing beard,
the forced apple smile, the thing bedecked.
More used to lettering altars, he had trouble
with the knees, getting the legs right,
its height from the ground,
the raised eyebrow, the twitching muzzle.
He didn't want anyone to see it
but duty…and it was a change from numerals
and it was good…and it had made him look.

Berkeley

There is a table in my study.
I see and feel it. It contains my pen,
paper, envelopes, and notebooks,
and if I wasn't there, but visiting
in the parish, it would happily
content itself with being, for a while.
Whether anything perceives it
in my absence, God or some spirit,
casting a curious glance at rosary,
crucifix, photograph of former vicar,
is a mystery. I don't really need
that idea for the desk still to be there
when I return. It props my arm, paper,
pen, allowing me to write a sermon
on how all things hold their own by leaning
on something infinitely greater.

Heart

I thought of other significant hearts:
Christ's, which in the Greek
would throw itself out;
Shelley's saved from fire and water
brought back to Bournemouth.
Now this child's. The doctor's hand
went far either side of it.
The pink tubes of the stethoscope
divined an unfamiliar sluicing.
Something in nature was too tight.
Something in Greek had gone wrong,
and although it made the old phrases
new – 'take heart', 'with all my heart'
for three days we put them aside
until the valve, tough as tripe, came right.

East

The first tug at the straw in the heck,
crisp mud, breath as smoke, the last
of the stock left out,
as the light breaks behind Skiddaw.
To paint it – the gentlest wash in the paint-box
and one hair of crimson.
It will not get much colder than this.
I know it is only us diving slow motion
round the sun, but since stories began
the sun has done the rising,
this month the palest.
Mattins is walking round the church
chanting, 'Dayspring.
Another beginning.'

South

We always pack to go south,
compressing what we are,
letting other things have a go at us for a while:
fruit, bays of warm sand,
fishing boats, light thin as muslin.
South is always a summer journey,
the annual pilgrimage, jostling.
Is that where the birds are off to
flying in shifting formation over Brown Moor?
A royal progress
leaving us to get on with winter?

North

We do up all our buttons against the wind,
walking on hidden paths beside fields
of long shadow. The lichen
bruises the stone walls.
What the wind can't shift
is here to stay.
We learn the earth's slow lessons,
are cautious of angels,
make sure the doors shut.

West

West is the end of the day
when the spade and the fork are
put in the barrow and wheeled away.
Overalls are dumped in the wash
and the table is ready.
Grace is warmth, light, peace.
Beyond the garden wall
in the glebe, the bullock
gives its last bellow and with
a gentle rearrangement of limbs
collapses front legs first
onto the frosted earth
waiting for the light from the east
and the cracking of the ice
to quench its thirst.

from

SELECTED POEMS

(1998)

Wittgenstein's Autumn

(Cambridge, 1947)

Is brown the word? Or should we say,
Harris Tweed, or leather of elbow patch?
Or the pale brown of dropped ash
at the edge of the hole in the essay?
Autumn ceases to be vegetable green,
and becomes a bold electric copper.
The sun performs the miracle
in its own particular language, which is
silently to turn the Backs Klimt-gold.

Bedtime Reading

The book was blue, had
viyella pages, encouraged
seriousness. I stretched
my soul so far, assuming
it would change the course of things
for good. It was a longing,
on which I put for eyes and ears,
miniature, rolled-up words:
night, cross, sheep, fears.

The First Poem

The first, real poem I ever wrote
is the one I want to lose, but can't.
They ask, 'when did you first start writing?'
and I say small things, with my father,
rhymes to ward off loneliness and murder,
much like Scheherezade. But the first
real poem committed in secret
is mixed up with a bench, high up on a balcony,
school paper, folded, folded again,
someone's sister, in velvet.
I told my poem for the first
and last time, everything.
Since then it's been attempts at truths,
competent, but nothing said from thirst
quenched by words. I dread
the folded paper coming back to me
like a carved heart grown too big on a tree.

Staying with Grandparents

She smoked du Maurier cigarettes
from the orange-box-type packet
in her pink rubber gloves
and dusted the dresser.
The ash lengthened until it leaned
and then she tapped it into the palm
of one glove and continued to dust
with the other.
                    He was sharpening
his deep-green pencil
in preparation for the crossword.
far away in a bedroom
with the leather cases, which had
labels stuck to them.

He taught me how to strip bark
off a stick, was particular about
the motion into and away from
a knot. Always away from yourself,
Louis Braille hadn't...

The penknife was my sharp friend.
On hot afternoons, by limestone walls,
we heard the convent bell,
had hours to be shocked by the lizard's
stillness, saw the heat melt upwards.

Hotel by the Sea

It should have been the sea,
but was only the pitch and put
and a raging throat. I sank
beneath a starched white tablecloth.
The heavy cutlery, the folded serviettes
and eventually the whole hotel
melted into a high temperature.
I found I was in a bed by a window
overlooking a church. The sound
of the radio news came along the corridor.
The chambermaid and the doctor,
and the big window onto the church:
and some nights it was bell-ringing practice.
I thought it was the after-life.
The doctor, with a French name,
sat on my bed and was God. God
had a case full of things, which
included a stethoscope.
Its winding up was perfect
like my tonsilled 'aargh'. Ever since,
I have wanted to see the doctor
again, but I find that God does not come,
quite so often, quite so far.

The Deserted Barracks

Here they laced the hot and silent tarmac
back into their boots for an hour of shouting.
Here they ducked into the Squash Court's
whiteness, to play for maximum male sweat,
exchanging boots for plimsolls on a splintery bench.
Here 'The Day thou gavest' ended, hanging
by a single chain from the chapel ceiling
The padre's blessing wide as a Sunday evening
swept away the pews. The memorials left
their wristwatch shapes on the creamy flaking walls.

This barracks has seen uniforms change
from the colour of butterflies
to the sludge in the deserted latrine
where the ceiling laths hang like ribs
and the cracked cistern boasts its origin
in Birmingham. A board with the admission price
for the Saturday film, still in heavy money,
advertises through the nettles.

I wonder why this fascinates me, perhaps
it's something to do with death, or the power of
rangey buddleias to push through cracks
in the empire, or is it a walking
through the ruins of my childhood,
knowing I can tread on them, and keep my
head in the sun, and walk away from it for good.

The Fourteenth Edition

It was all there in one long
dog-eared stretch.
What wasn't there, wasn't knowledge.
The rest was just a rumour on the air.
Knowledge was heavy, each volume
by itself, needed two hands,
the whole set was immovable.
We went to lift out knowledge now and then,

when something great like Alexander
had to be researched. For punishment
I wrote out the article on bricks.
The backs of all the 23, plus index,

was the only decoration in the room.
I'm beginning to think that
the alphabetical abbreviations,
broken, brief, escaping from the text,

kindled a flame of poetry,
A to ANNO, VASE to ZYGO,
journeys which explained nothing,
but signalled other airy things to know.

Stamp Album

It began in Abyssinia
on wet afternoons
while the stamps unpeeled in the sink.
I turned the pages
of a concentrated oblong world,
never quite focusing.
Only now, when the swaps have
been pressed for all those years
in the Book of Daniel
do I look at them again,
with a magnifying glass
also my grandfather's.
I now can lift a stamp
up to the light and see
its watermark of wars and famines.
In Deutsches Reich 'Mark' is
overlaid with 'tausend', overlaid
with 'millionen'. In Serbia
there is a man with a braided cap
and a high-necked dress jacket.
There was a lot of military braid
and medals when this collector
first folded and licked a stamp hinge,
and the world ended far away
with a bearded gaze in Zanzibar.

Cleaning the Shoes

To anyone passing
(I tend to be in the yard)
they would see the cleaning of shoes.
For me it is a daily remembrance
of the holiday where I bought the brushes.
Holywell was the place, and we picnicked
on the hill, and I carved on one brush
'ON', and on the other brush 'OFF'.

Holywell is near Chester
where I once stayed with the nuns.
They wore light blue,
one had a father who was dying,
and all this comes back to me
as I twist off the lid of the polish.
Its smell brings to me the nuns of Chester.

'What are you doing?'
'Oh, just cleaning the shoes.'

Last of the Line

I have a way
(it's probably the best thing I do)
of getting a hand in a shoe
and patting the brush in the polish
and rubbing it round,
first one side, then the other,
then toe, then heel.
I notice the particular scuffs
and creases. I think I can tell
how those who wear them are getting on
from the shape of their shoes, how they are
leaning, and the pace of things.
My father did the same, but with
a different lung-filled breathing,
and he'd use the occasion to talk
about the stages of life's changes.
Perhaps I'll be the last of the line
of the great shoe cleaners,
newspaper fire-lighter twisters,
piler up of coin-ziggurats,
whispering adding-uppers,
stuffer of wet shoes.

John Keats

Don't breathe on me – it comes like Ice.
KEATS' LAST WORDS

It's why at certain times
we pick that book,
casting for a mood, a line,
that no one else has managed
quite like that. He leaves whole bits
of life completely satisfied in words.
Autumn of course, and melancholy,
the heraldry of shadow on the skin,
shades of darkness, juices, scents
that send us back to check
a memory. He was dressed in poetry,
sat to it, made a life and death of it:
the old Guy's alchemist
turning ice back into breath.

Gauguin

The weight of the whole body
on the one arm, leaning
into the earth, so the earth
and the arm are part of
each other, not just in colour
but in blood, in a state of loving
where flowers grow from the head,
and there's no sky for heat to escape.

Watercolour

(Owen Merton 1887-1931)

Trusting the sliding wet
and mixing it with coloured earth
you made the fire and air
of southern France and Africa.

The river in San Antonin
drove through your studio
destroying all you owned.
The authorities, chucked
the sodden, curling works.
That left you just the bits
of paper on your hospital bed
on which you scribbled
faces of the saints.

Leaving the bedside glass
a long, dark night away,
you took the only thing to hand
and practising for the end,
tried light on light.

Saint Jerome in his Study

(from Antonello da Messina)

This translator owns a peacock.
You'd think it would be a distraction, but
perhaps it screams at the difficult words
to save him doing it. 'Him' is St Jerome.
He is on at the Bible, and has got himself set up.
For reasons of concentration, he has made
a room inside a room, and the work begins
where the rooms stop. Any minute the room could
swivel to a bedroom, pushed by a stage hand
between scenes. It doesn't move,
nor does the writer, nor does his hat,
nor does the crimson gown, nor does the peacock.
The writer is concentrating.
There is a real commitment from hat,
through sleeve, to the page, and back again.
His world is Latin. Glimpse the beauty
through the windows, brown hills, bird circling sky,
but only we can see that. The writer is looking
to see what he can bend to the latin
in his open cupboard, with the bonsais
in chalices. The depths of the house
are the depths of his mind, I suppose.
We blink from one world to the other.
Writing is something you do alone in a room,
with a peacock always just about to peck the grain.

Selborne, some 29th of Junes

Dragon-flies have been out some days

> giant tulip-tree
> > old fashioned sweet-peas
> beech trees in heat haze
> > gazebo, iron pyrites

Dragon-flies move like an architect's

> rule, each zip taking its
> > whole length along with it.
> Box hedge, lavender,
> > zigzag, insects.

Dragon-flies helicopt the pond

> with blue, upright wings
> > tubes of electricity.
> A beech leaf drops in the wood wistfully
> > like a junk bobbing on the China sea.
> Cherry tree shades a seminar
> > four spread out with notes
> on the subject of ecology.

Dragon-flies come out of their amelia-state

> (observed by the Reverend
> > Gilbert White
> aha!
> > saint of the close look,
> staying put, notebook)

Thomas Merton's Cambridge
(1933)

71, Bridge Street
is now opposite a bookshop
over a camera shop
beside a bookbinders
(which was there when he was).
You can't really get a good look at the flat
except by stepping back
on the opposite side of the road
against a record shop window.
Looking up to the first floor window,
there is a 'TO LET' sign.
(This is of course for devotees,
who else would want such detail?)
So you could rent it
but the pile of rubbish
swept into a corner of the empty room
would remind you
of how much he hated the place.
It was 1933,
King Kong was on at the Central
and *The Tempest* at the Tivoli.
Stumbling back to the room
above the 'Athletic Stores and Hairdressers'
after a bull-nosed journey from London,
was, in the end, no one's idea of fun.
Even the river was seeing double
in the dark months of that year.

The Hermitage, Gethsemani

(1964)

And yet what he would come to
see as sin, was the culture God
grew warm in. Each room had its place
and the undergraduate cartoons
struck a chord with Chuang T'zu.
There is the camera, the books,
the records, which I have
to stand up against the window
of your soul to see. The difference
is that this has the icons,
and the slow noise of a fire
gently crackling to the internal jazz.

The Martyrdom of Saint Polycarp

My last early light, last stretch
of being upheld by earth,
last knocking of my soul
against its boundary wall.
Soon, guesswork will be overrun by sight.
I am the starved animal's only lair.
Its sharp hug will be cross-matched
with a welcoming Christ's.
Farewell, here. Welcome, there.
Lion keeper, take me to the fair!

For Frances Horovitz

I think of you
walking in Roman territory
picking up images
to make a necklace,
homing like a buzzard
on one resilient, named flower
in a crevice of The Wall.
For feathers and snow,
no one better.
You put on and took off the landscape
like a tight sweater.

Emily Brontë's Off-days

Was it always like this, or did
the crinoline have holes, the fingernails
bitten edges? Were there long periods
of nothing much at all, knocking
one stair's dust down to the next,
and no words. Days when the graves went blind
by a sigh on a pane of glass, and the yew branch
scratted an empty afternoon mind.
When you decided you couldn't be bothered
to go bent head-first onto the moors,
but just wanted to stay at home and dream something
unimaginative, selfish, stereotyped.
Between bouts of red-hot genius, to be
ordinary, relaxed, so that I could have
a conversation without shaking
with suppressed emotion.
Will heaven reveal this, or will it smooth
the gradient so much, it won't be you?

Sappho

An icon, full-face, of you,
but a shadow of doubt
and stylus to lip
puts you among poets,
not saints. Brow-bridged nose
catches the scent of what stirs
below the picture.
Green stylus, robe, tablet, ties,
fragments of poems,
I saw you in Edinburgh
small, poised between hiding
and revealing, secrets.

A Dismantling Job

We had grown accustomed to the green shroud,
covering the west end of the cathedral,
while the stone-masons tapped above the crowd,
and the glaziers pieced the panes of glass,
thirsty for light, back into the roundel.
But look, they are beginning the slow unwrapping
of that vast back: first one shoulder,
then the next, slipping from the metal tubes
they had grown used to. Across the close,
we hear that particular clink of scaffold,
and thud of board that is the tuning
for a dismantling job. Some day it will step
completely out of its awkward dress,
and will stand up as it was,
hungry for the sun to bless. The men
in hard hats up-end their barrows
bag the chisels and levels, take a night's rest.

Wisteria

Planners ask the question:
   'Who put this thirty foot
   wisteria into the ground, and why?'

Historians recount the name makers:
   one 18th century, american anatomist, Caspar
   Wistar.

Botanists use words
   like 'recemes' for the thing
   that holds flowers like beads on a string.

Lovers writhe with the climber
   in the bleached purple T-shirt
   causing a wild hurt,

which leaves, the one who reflects
   on its soft breeze finery
   wafting from the 8th Dynasty.

Peacock

You crazy limousine! There is
nothing less like an argument
or a sermon, but I'll describe you
in three parts, nevertheless.

I

Your head and neck show such caution,
are not relaxed, think in slices.
You are topped by a fine comb,
are aware, preen your petrol blue duvet.
For a man, I must say, you put it on.

II

Your middle is full of contradiction,
held together under the title,
'Quite Ordinary Hen'.

III

Your train though by all accounts
should be in Paradise, and perhaps it is,
pecking the buttercups. You
Xanadu of birds. You beauty.
I gave my ballgown away some time ago
otherwise I would have filled my palm with grain
and enticed you to dance.
You are so 20s, twitchy, so
accessory.

A Nun on the Platform

She seems in place here,
as much as in the convent,
self-contained, neat.
You could hardly call it luggage.

No frantic balancing of cups,
but like a swan, which also
has no hands for magazines,
she stands complete.

No intermediate, half unsureness,
no drawing kids back from the edge,
or disappointment over missing,
or expectation of arrival

of a train, leans her,
like the rest of us, out of true.
We are all some distance from our roots
on this platform, but she seems at home,

as her Sisters will be
in the over large garden
reaching for tall fruits,
their thoughts ripening for pardon.

Seeing a nun on a platform
gives the day a jolt,
like an act of kindness,
or a pain that halts.

Between

This between is staring down at sea,
     churned and frothed
and spumed colossally
     into individual maelstroms of broth.

I touch the painted blistering of rust,
     and mirror varnish of the rail,
and see the random gust
     make canvas covers flail.

A wind-stiff face can only take
     so many spray-flecked
moments. Enough to make
     occasion to reflect

'what's gone is gone', and cliffs
     and long-rod fishers
on the quay, are only if's
     as full of air as wishes.

So for the length of time it takes
     to find the wind too much,
I follow shadowed ridge
     on shadowed ridge

until my eye returns
     to a still but moving prow,
which makes of all before and after
     a momentary 'now'.

Dusk

Acrobatic swallows zim it
from wire to eave through a
circus tent of dusk,
compass tails looping
the loop until light
is pushed to the limit.

The Wedding

Is there something I can do
to give this wedding such a push
that it will last for ever?

What conjuror can squeeze
so many aspirations
through such a small ring?

If I was him
I would want to get out of those
absolutes as quickly as out of the suit,

because his bride, like everyone's,
has caught the colour of the sun
this afternoon.

My Best Hatt

Noe I have not so much but that I can dispose of it by word of
mouth...my best Hatt I give to my brother Philip.

(Will of THOMAS TRAHERNE,
Proved at London, October 22, 1674)

Was the problem, after all your catch
of wonders the Hatt you'd only sometimes worn
might lack another head to match?

Was it a best Hatt day when the faces
of the Ledbury youth and newly born
showed signs of angels' traces?

Was the Hatt the one you wore when the sun
smoothed its hand across the corn
when your sabbath work was done?

And what of the second-best hat,
was that too forlorn
to give away? I would have liked that.

Only the best Hatt then could
take its place to adorn
the final distribution of your goods:

your good, your singular good, your best Hatt
which became your brother Philip's turn
to wear and wonder at.

Grandma Moses

Life is what you make it, always has been, always will be.

And she makes it what she wants,
wrapped in a crocheted shawl
looking with steel-rimmed glasses
through the window which is swathed
in the cleanest bobbled lace.
The view is a white palisade,
and the pear-blossom trees
up the Hoosick valley to the hills.
A red house, a yellow house,
nothing untoward, God's quilt.
There is a road that winds around a corner
into nothing to fear, and people are
never more than this high, with no gripes,
and always engaged, even the ones
tapping the hours away with clay pipes.
Life is how you paint it, like a child
she saw no shadows on the stripes.

A Botticelli Nativity

Before the entry of the Kings,
their horses, caparisoned and fettled,
the peacock got itself settled

on a crumbling wall,
where the stones sprout flowers
through long Italian hours.

Much lather at the bit is slavered,
and steam coils off the stallions' bared
backs. We enter at the point where

discussion across empty saddles
is hushed, and one of the Kings unfurls,
from beneath a golden band, a head of curls.

This gives an opportunity for drapery
to swing in the direction of a baby,
ruling from a crimson knee.

The peacock spreads its cards
behind its back. The Kings unleash
their homage. All the haberdashery is hushed.

This Medici Bethlehem is squaring up
to its Christ, with the beautiful and shy
Madonna, and the peacock preens the sky.

The Ruthwell Cross

This Christ heads out to the Atlantic
and is battered by winds and weather.
Carved in majesty with simple strokes
nothing more subtle would have held together.

This is no delicate Christ.
This was set up to astonish,
and on this the gulls could
scan for fish, waves could crash.

Whoever carved this, knew
Christ in glory;
a match for the sun,
the hero of the story.

They set it in earth to
reach to the centre, up to
the heavens, across to the edges.
Within its spars were wrapped

the marvels of creation,
such as even the mystic
Magdalen, could share with
the Christ of the edgeless Atlantic.

Abbey Ruins

Until now I've been stuffy
about ruins: symbols of a past
unable to reach into the present,
and I might be so again, but,
this afternoon I saw three girls
slip their links of iron, and
move in sacred space like dancers.
They were unopposed by altar, door,
or roof. One smoothed the stone
as if it was a face. They walked
their full height with natural flair.
The ruin, like a shell cracked open, lay
aghast at their experiment with air.

A Postcard from Lake Trasimene

Remember this island?
Well, it's still here,
though I haven't the energy to visit it.
Yours, Michael.

I've visited that island since, in my mind
a thousand times, and it remains
as fresh as on that one and only morning.

We slept in a boathouse,
cobwebs on the chandlery,
and I read *The Little Flowers*
of St Francis.

Francis stood upside down,
rolled in the snow, for
forty days fasted on this island,
eating only the bread of the gospels.
He read them off the menu of the lake
where the whitebait glinted in the dusk.

What else do I remember?
You wore glasses.
We boiled water on a candle
waiting for the boat to
take us back to the mainland.
I still have the book.
Francis still inspires me.
We haven't met since.

I think if I found myself as near as you,
it wouldn't be lack of energy
that kept me away. It would be to do
with preferring the memory.

'Afterwards, at this place where St Francis
had observed such an amazing fast,
God worked many miracles through his merits.'

I wonder what you're doing now?
The Law, I think, or the Foreign Office.
I'm working through the miracles.
I'd love to meet and see if what was
pivotal for me, was that, or just
another place for you. I wouldn't judge,
in fact I'd be surprised if providence
worked in twos. To meet would be
to find out other moments
meaningful to you.

Stinsford Churchyard

In the distance, traffic; under the yew tree
silence; on the yew tree, a few red berries,
each squashy as a heart. About the church
Hardy would have things to say
of a building nature: the pointing,
and mouldings, but also how the dusk
lays everything out on the ground
half of itself again.
The hoary lichen on the table tombs
follows chisel and pommel
along inscriptions. Weathered names
and dates and chosen texts, seem
in Hardy's churchyard, so resonant of story.

Vindolanda

Cats in the car park, sicilian, lyrical,
shelter with the yellow poppies.
The shop. The museum. Then the climb up
to the fort, drawn by skylarks
piping prep school Latin. Here is
the crust, time has not scoured off:
the stone's shape, the helmet sky.
Red and white wands, and labels,
posted into growing piles of millennia
pass on rumours of a sandal, a fence.
The martin's pronged swerve, learnt in Italy,
winds the cogs for the long parabola home.
We have to imagine knuckle-bones, Virgil, dogs.

A Roll of Honour, Steep Church

'Taylor, Thomas, Tucker, Tyrell'
a proper epitaph, to end up
as a name among other names, like a plant,
or a station. This dim, north aisle
bites off a corner of quiet to calm
a restless spirit, which tramped from
one Ordnance Survey map to another before lunch.
It hit the uphill hard, rooting for something
beneath the soil. It opened letters
like a pigeon breaking from a holly tree.
Words came to an end. The spirit's owner
hung his jacket up. His pipe's chewed
bakelite turned white. The gate swung,
banging the roll-call: 'Taylor, Thomas,
Tucker, Tyrell...'

Monteverdi Vespers

The ermined Senate and their Doge
in chisel-toed, block-heeled shoes,
gathered their pugs off the golden gondolas
and made money as they walked
across the square. Monteverdi
weaved his manuscript, warm as bread,
between them. It was Ash Wednesday.
He was worried that the music
was less stark, less penitential
than the sackcloth day deserved.
The pigeons flew and fell
to the crumbs and the bankers' drone,
while inside the church, counterpoint
rose from the chequered, marble floor
to lick the inside of the dome, and fall
to ricochet with the next piece of the score.

A Quaker Sitting

He sits, relaxed, on a hard chair,
legs crossed, waiting
for a testimony to uncoil within
or not. Silence will more than do.

His desire to speak, links
with the store of words he has
gathered over the years from books
and humane conversations.

Some words he will send back as too bold,
too much of the tall hat and the breeches.
Others will not be shaken off and come with
the wisdom of long silences.

If I were a painter of the Primitive American School
after a period of silent preparation myself,
I would work on the contact of chair and bare boards,
and the space between leaned head and rafter.

Then it would be the turn of the ungainly pockets,
and the holding of the elbow in one hand,
and the chin in the finger and the thumb.
Something about the cut of this prayer

reminds me of the conscientious objector
and the Ambulance Corps, frugality,
evening classes at The Settlement
and household pain. I would title it 'Wisdom Heaped'.

The Castelbarco Tomb, Verona
painted by John Ruskin, 1869

Such a big building to paint all in one
which is why he did it in bits
out of the glare of the sun. Lyrical tiles,
rooms like boxes in a chest of drawers,
'the ogee curve of the apex
the cusps giving inward weight
to the great stone flanks', washed by
a quiet Italian light. It was
as big and complicated as himself:
poet, painter, prophet, builder.
He had at times to paste himself together
after he had flown apart in gloom.
Sometimes things were just too big for him.
He saw too much, and so returned
to pencil and a line, to letter and a word.
But he did piece it all together in the end
so we could see what it was all about,
and there it stands in the Hall, a jigsaw
finished, glowing with its
umber ins and outs, a tomb, a metaphor.

The Common Loon

Against the power-boat's soulless
roar, manically
skidding its careless
moneyed figures on the lake,
the loon waits. In the spaces
left it, early, late,
the loon keeps warning:

'I am all that's left
of the ancient sounds',
and its prophetic tremolo
goes deeper and deeper
more and more liquid
into the lake's length.

The Barn, Ontario

I seldom go in barns now,
have to think my way back
through the wide summer doors,
but the setting and the lean of this one
make its outside something to remark.

He said, 'The longer the winter, the
bigger the barn.' This one's height
was set to survive three feet of snow.
Now, bleached black like an old fire,

some plans have sprung out from the nails,
and the corrugated iron roof has left
edges for the storms to lift, and
the winter is neither here nor there.

Its purpose gone, it has nothing now to do
but lean, and drop planks like teeth.
until at last its absence will make
the landscape seem more bare, more vast.

Cabot Head Lighthouse, Ontario

The girl in the lighthouse
 swats a fly
  with a lazy hand.
   Salt-white boards,
    simple things,
     suitable, purged.
    The girl
   has skin as smooth
  as birch bark.
 Mute waves
crash on the rock.
 Poisoned ivy
   plans its route along the path.
    Here is the chart,
     here is the huge lamp,
      here are the winding
       stairs.
    The hours are
      poised.
   On a shelf
  a boiled rattlesnake
 quietly coiled
would take no other shape
 than the clear jar
  would let it
   in the liquid
    which had drowned
     both rattle and bite.

A Priest with the Bible

I begin with Ruth because
in the dusk of the barley field
she shines out between
the Book of Judges and the 1st Book of Samuel,
as a woman of struggle
and commitment. She turned
her life into a poem, and was the
mother of the father of a poet.

...move quickly on
to the Song of Songs,
with its ramparts and gazelles,
cinnamon, frankincense,
and its sheer hard won delight
between he and she.

I do not forget sad Hannah
drunk with torment,
and her gift of a son,
Samuel.

I stand in envy at Wisdom
with all her clever and beautiful children
who answer the questions, spot the clues,
mend the fuses, see into the heart of things.
Wisdom's family has both a weaver,
and a sewer on of buttons,
is not perturbed by snow
falling secretly in the night.

...recall some of the surprise births:
Sarah's, Elizabeth's, Mary's:
and don't forget the words of Jesus,
'Who is my mother and my brother?'

Memo:
the widow of Nain's son,
Simon Peter's mother-in-law
Martha's sister
Lot's wife
Cain's brother

I plead that we do not skip lightly through
the genealogies, for they speak
volumes as well as generations.
Let us not rush the genealogies
or laugh at them,
for noses and hair and the ways
of laying a fire and cleaning shoes
will persist and mark us as
her daughter and his son.
And as wisdom dances and
slices through the time line,
and as miracles set fire
to particular moments,
and Rachel and Jacob meet by the well
among the sheep, the invisible
strings of family weave, shall we say,
a context of love, to catch the pains
when they come in the middle of the night.

When it comes to it,
not many others will do,
which is why David wept for Absalom,
his enemy and son, and why
at the cross of Jesus
stood Mary, his mother.

A Priest in a New Parish

The river draws me, always, running
like fingers through my hair. It leaps out
unexpectedly; makes itself available
just to be heard: its voice over chalk.
Sunday afternooners catch the current
with bits of bread for ducks to scoop.
The swans live in a world of their own.
This same Saxon riddle of water has
been here since flint was first
put next to brick, and kings
were shut in dusty boxes, and books
went to seed along the shelves.
Rivers are largely why any of us are
anywhere in particular. They choose us.
Struggling to settle in, to find my voice,
my place, I listen to this water's
mute capacity to sing.

A Priest at the Crematorium

Outside the West Chapel,
I was flipping through the prayers
in final preparation for the service
of someone who had cycled
the groceries round on a bike.
The family in awkward suits,
were nipping their fags, before
stepping onto the automatic
mourners' walkway. It was
sticky hot. To eye the coffin in
I looked up, and towards
the East Chapel there flowed,
like candles on a river,
twenty upright women
in saris; their veils catching
and releasing the sun.
They were so graceful, as if
there was no such thing as death.

A Priest at the Door

I sit at the door of the church
and see who comes in and who goes out.
They don't hand anything in
like they used to, animals or grain.
I don't have to receive anything
to put on the altar, or pass anything
to my assistant to be slaughtered
and the blood drained and flung.
I am grateful for that, not
having been brought up to it.
Instead they get books and papers
snippets of news, and the magazine.
Somebody else does all that.
I have no ephod to divine the truth,
no incense to burn, no curtain
to close behind me. I have only the agony
of knowing I have little,
and the slow job of resisting
any attempt to make it more, because
in my mind's eye I have the eye of the needle,
and how easy it is for even
licked thread to miss getting through.

George Herbert's Last Sunday

He could see the instrument
from where he lay. Illness
kept pushing it further away
until the day the cows
returning to the byre
passed the faithful going to Evensong
and the bell tolled. It was his custom
to hear the bell inside the church,
but today he heard it from his bed.
It rang out, 'Praise does not depend
on you alone. Feel dispensable.'
The lute called him to cross
the lengthening room to play 'Sunday'
to the tune of a madrigal.

A Priest in a Bookshop

I go to find some arcane, 1920s
books on St John of the Cross,
but on the way down I see and smell
some other things, not of the period.
A bird beats against the bars of my stomach
with handwriting like Anaïs Nin's.
I leave my arm among the Hasidim,
and put a shell to my ear
to hear the sea thrashing on the shore.
It takes me some time, skirting astrology,
to get to the spines of the books
I am familiar with. High up the ladder,
or bending my head to the floor,
what am I searching for? Words
that are waiting for me, charms against
the menace of fungus in the cracks,
and the delicate skulls of birds.

A Priest at Prayer

From prayer to prayer involves
a dwindling, a way of being
that accounts for weariness, a regular
drawing in and letting out of breath;
the planting of a word and its forgetting,
a close examination of what is there
until it isn't, a candle flame beating air,
love meeting Love before the house wakes up;
space body-shaped, time vacated,
the passive tense, a waiting to receive,
out-of-bounds of what is right
or wrong, subject to being surprised
by God on briefest sight.

My Bike

I prop it up, steady it,
pull my trousers out of my socks,
and knock to enter into
a death, or any other
of life's routine shocks.
'Bring it in'. I carry it
like an awkward animal and
introduce it to the shoes and shopping,
where it waits.
              The talk ranges
from the now, to the past, to the weather
mostly skirting eternity.
I carry it out into new air,
where it takes the strain
in the pedals. We weave between ducks
and day-outers, until it hits the garage
almost horizontal, like a laid hedge,
among bits of hose, tired footballs,
the rusty sledge. It sleeps where it falls.

from

PIECING TOGETHER

(2005)

First Thing

One young deer
on the path to the wood
then following
three more together.
How it stopped me
even inside the house
my shirt in my hands
every bit of my body
wired up for watching
every bit of theirs radar
for the merest blink.
Air rigid between us,
they moved first,
nobly, silently,
sensuous as waking.

This Meadow, a Soul

Left to grow beautiful
the grassy heads do gentle talking,
and as a whole move to an unseen hand,
this way and that. The size of a soul
is like this, just let to be, to breathe,
to bathe in its own space. God has every
confidence in it, resisting continual visits
to check on how it's going. It's going all right.
Occasionally a secret breath unseen
blows joy across its face
and in return the soul picks up its skirts
and makes long swathes in meadow lengths of space.

Valley Road, Louisville

Thanks be to God
that sometimes we can
walk in Eden. Quiet
in the morning, I catch
the shadow and the sun,
so neither hurt.
I know there's a world
elsewhere, but am allowed this one.
Whatever the six-fold lips
of the lily say, they say it kindly.
Trees there are in plenty
arching like Blake's tall angels
over me, each a blessing, none
bearing the troublesome apple.

Brighton Pier, 10 A.M.

It's quiet at the moment.
The chips are still their pale potato selves.
The *Brasso*'s whitening on the ornaments,
and someone's counting something on the shelves.

An early group of three, breathe
the freedom of not land, not sea.
There's no Fortune Teller in the booth.
The deckchairs, in their horizontal piles, are free.

The Galloping Steeds are motionless.
The smells of vinegar and Candy Floss
incubate in silence
anticipating their release.

With everything just that little out of reach,
I'm given space to lean against the rail,
and watch a girl tread the sliding beach,
each loping step leaving a long trail.

It was as if she'd
waited all the way from Birmingham
to lift a cupped hand of the sea,
and to cast it, randomly.

Mud Revisited

(for May Badman)

I was stumbling across a field
with the magazine in hand
reading the published poem. 'It was there!'
My first. What was I doing in the field?
I was ascending with the larks.
Cyclostyled and stapled, the cover
the colour of blancmange, and the poem
was there. Why should it make a difference?
It wasn't a big poem as poems go,
but I'd sent it into the great unknown,
and half forgotten about it.
What had become of the poem was anyone's guess,
but in the dark unpredictable 'no' of publishing
some unforgettable eye had said 'yes'.

Prayer and the Hair Salon

I am a priest of Winchester.
A candle flickers in the upstairs cell.
I watch the snow fall on the heads
of the passers-by. My prayer is soft
as snow. It does little but
cover the ground, and the candle shivers.

Opposite and down is a Hair Salon.
I can see the long napes of necks
as the hair is lifted, curled, and cut,
or pinned with papers like bookmarks.
I pray, and because of the cold
hug my already tight cloak tighter. Why?

Strange contradictions don't have
answers always. It happens so.
What do I pray for: that the heat
could be shared, that I should get a
haircut, that they will put down
their scissors and pray?
Not yet. Someone higher looks at me,
and says 'poor fool'; or perhaps,
'all you need to do is stay'.

The Priest in the Pulpit

Will it last, this opening of the heart
to the Word, or will the new ways,
the film, the television, the e-mail,
dislodge us from the art of oratory?
Climbing the steps, taking off the paper clip,
remembering not to put it in my mouth,
the text, the Greek, the joke, the text again,
all this, O God, you know, as well as asking you
to make all things, especially the haste,
respectable. As the spiral notebooks rust
along the shelves, who knows how a word
in the thickest of the sermon's stickiest part,
might just have winged its way into the heart
of one young stranger there, and taken roost.

Meeting St John of the Cross

I would look for signs of weather
at the edges of your clothes, your hands
for the way you hold your pen, and put it down.
I would glance to notice shifts of sun and shadow
of the alternating poetry and prose in you.
I would be curious, acute to sense
such mundane sacraments. The drawing,
small and aerial of Christ, seen
from the Father's desperate height, and the voice
which reached down songs from such tall trees,
would pose questions, as unanswerable
as why the storks so love the towers of Avila.

Augustine Baker talks to the Nuns of Cambrai

So much to say. The Cambrai days were long
and the nuns didn't have to attend,
which meant they didn't, except one,
and then one by one, until there were ones
all over Christendom. The first words though,
the early tentative drafts, the birdsong
while the hill above the trees stood still
in the mist, what of those, before they were books,
when there were only a few words and those
the same: 'silence, solitude, love, and love again'?

The Healer

I asked her what she did, and
she said, 'healer'. We talked
about the central nervous system
and how I wasn't looking after mine.
There was no grille or wooden box
but it had the air of a confessional.
The music was about to start again
which left no time for absolution
in the conventional sense. I think
she might have been an angel, for
I have the indent of a wing along my side.

Caedmon's Song

Wind through the consonants,
air through the vowels,
starlight through the planks,
God in the outhouse.

That's where the poem began.
I saw it from the B & B
looking across from the barn
to the ruin of the Abbey.

Among the cattle, the air
in the silence, the wind
in the dust, I heard you
before breakfast, and made

this song of it. God
of the nearer presence
and the long view
I saw you, and I sing of you.

For Pete Laver

(1947-1983)

After all these years
here comes the elegy.
We walked the long path from the church
to the burial ground, not quite sure
whether to talk or not. It was warm
and bright. (Twenty years on
it is drizzling).
                    You were so funny.
The first time we met, you were perusing
the headstones in our churchyard
having earlier backed your car
into the River Derwent near Wordsworth's house.

Here is your grave, the smallest of stones
like a bit off someone else's. Perhaps
someone nicked it for you, that would figure.
The lettering has almost gone so I trace it
with my finger like Braille, 1947,
we began together...

It was a warm day in summer,
so many poets, so many young people,
women in gay dresses, so much beauty
and memories of laughter. So,
why then
after all these years this
uncontrollable checking of tears?

Heart on Pilgrimage

My heart goes walking
to the ancient places,
Jerusalem, Lindisfarne,
holy places all. Prayer
can take me there:
to the foot of the cross,
to the edge of the world,
to the eye of the Buddha,
the muezzin, the kestrel
hovering over the motorway,
and my heart can go thwack
to another heart as quick
as silicon, but
bringing it back...

The Church of the Holy Sepulchre, Jerusalem

She is in love with someone, I can tell.
When she sits, she sits alone and still.
Her shrouded face, encompassing profound denials,
surfaces in light, and says, 'I will'.

Her movement speaks of shadows, edges,
and who it is she loves is not found here,
not there, but moving from the centre
of her longing, is with her everywhere.

Qumran, Cave no.4

Despite all the talk of the Prince of Light,
this is the centre of the coolest darkness.
The light which on the outside
makes a dust of stones, here only angles in,
and the scrolls rolled up in jars, sleep:
sleeping and waiting for the chance eye
of a Bedouin boy. Why now, why then:
these scrolls about so fervently
expected things, waiting, waiting?

Mea Shearim, Jerusalem

On the shutters and the crumbling walls
ripped notices, only words,
flap in the cold, late Sabbath wind.
I peep into heaven, and there
the bright neon strip-lighting
glazes the black and white Hasidim
twiddling hair and stroking beards
in the House of the Lord.

High up and diagonally across the road,
a daughter of Jerusalem
eyes her brothers through the chink
of makeshift wooden slats.
They sway and nod and say so well
the things they have to pray
on the terraced sides of heaven.
Long after her bedtime, she thinks
what is it to be a sister, a woman, a bride?

A Boat on Iona Bay

So many times my pen has tried that boat:
how she rests in the water as if nothing
could bother her; how much she enjoys just floating,
waiting release from the anchor.
The slight laying back of the masts and rigging
is very satisfactory. Happy in herself, breathing
as if she might have just been drawn
through the tight neck of a bottle, and raised
and rigged full-sail, upright.

St Columba's Bay, Iona

Among the bones of seagulls
          and of kings
and with all this muffled, nibbled turf
      even the sea's gone quiet,
          imagine that!

In respect for such unusual tenderness
      it wasn't difficult
   to walk the long way home
cradling a crab shell in my hand;

leaving behind, on this occasion
   the weight of intricate stones.
      It was with a light step
         that afternoon
         I made it home.

With Miggy at Skelwith Force

This was where my father brought me,
and now in bringing you
I sense a change in scale and clarity.

Water eases from a petrol smoothness
into a broth so fierce the rocky sides
seem moving up and not the water down.

A fish falls upwards flashing black
against the bridal veil of spume,
and at the edge a single harebell shivers.

All this meant danger for a father and a son,
but now, with he away and I grown out of sandals,
there's no longer any reaching up for rail or hand.

I know a different sort of peace,
something about holding the wonder
in a new-found capacity to understand.

'the infinite sweetness of the Greek text'

SIMONE WEIL

Dear Simone, I know what you mean
but only now, at last.
I found my student text, disregarded,
naively underlined in biro.
It was the pressure of exams.
I re-read Peter's words to Jesus,
You are the Christ:
four words in Greek
but stripped of English cloy,
and shining separately bright. The Greek
spread through me like a dye,
(and would you understand this too?)
came to rest, not only through the language,
but in the precision of their being true.

Ibn Abbad woke early

(11 September 2001)

Ibn Abbad woke early, put on
his patched garment, turned to God
and said, *Peace be to us, and to all, this
day.*

Rabbi Schmelke of Nikolsburg,
when a rich and distinguished man
tried to make him look ridiculous,
read the forty-first psalm, and
translated verse eleven, *By this
I know that you delight in me:
my enemy will suffer no ill because of me.*

Father Louis in his American hermitage
wrote to Abdul Aziz, *Let us
have great love for truth, and open our hearts
to the spirit of God our Lord and Father,
Compassionate and Merciful.*

All three went to Paradise,
Ibn Abbad, Rabbi Schmelke of Nikolsburg,
and Father Louis, and sat to eat
at the same table. They drank the water of life
and ate the meat of friendship. Whenever
their cups ran dry or their plates were empty
a little Nazarene came by and filled them up.
Who are you? they said.
I am Jesus, son of Mary. Can I sit awhile?
Be our guest, they said.

As they sat, the ground beneath them shook,
their faces paled and their eyes were filled
with knowledge, and with grief. *Today,*
said Jesus, *they will hate more and
love more, than on any other day since
the world began. Hold hands,*

and ask our God to speak to us
in Spirit. And there they sat
in love and prayer, all day, all day,
Ibn Abbad, Rabbi Schmelke of Nikolsburg,
Father Louis, and Jesus, Mary's son.

and their silence was more profound than words
and their communion was most eloquent
and they willed the world to peace

After a long time they opened their eyes,
and there were only three at the table.
Jesus, Mary's son, had gone,

    had gone to join some other hands in love
    sit by some other beds of pain
    pray with some other desperate men
    break for some other hearts the loaf
    share with some other faiths the way

and that goes on today
unceasing in his care to see beyond the robes
of different length, and hue, and cloth,
the common beating heart, and to mark again
as on the Bethlem night, the angels' call:
Peace on the earth, goodwill to all, to all.

The Mug

We'd seen them in the Ashmolean:
Cistercian Ware. I thought of Rievaulx,
and asked if you could make the same design:
black glaze, tallish, the waisted shape.
You did, and when you were in hospital
that was the mug I chose to sip from,
in the early hours, imagining you gone.
I turned you, and turned you, until,
putting you down beside the lamp,
I was amazed at how the black glaze shone

On thinking of not throwing the old Road Map away

I've read it upside down, right way up,
with glasses, without, driving and stationary,
marked in green felt-tip pen the way to The Dell,
via Raymond Rd, Gresham Rd, Atherley Rd,
put a red circle round the Grosvenor Square Car Park
so I could get to the Art Gallery through Watts Park.
What isn't marked, but should be, in gold,
is the boot that turned up on the side of the
Chandlers Ford by-pass just before the roundabout
leading into Bassett Avenue. It was there
like a Monopoly piece, every time we passed
on the way to the General, to watch and wait
and wonder about a brain being mended,
a life being sewn back into place. When it was,
and we went back together to the shops,
to buy curtains or some other stuff,
the boot had gone. It was there, like God,
or the surgeon, or a good friend, just long enough.

I pollarded am

I pollarded am.
My elbows ancient are,
but my hair, which
out of my neck does grow,
the head hacked off having been,
is young, absurdly, rubbery so.
O so ancient my chest and hips
pressing the legs of me, now stumps,
deep into underground.

Why do they this pollarding do?
One day, no doubt,
thus and thus did some king say.
So from the folly of an autumn cut,
it came to must be so.

They say in China this they do to feet,
in other countries, minds,
and others, souls. Thus nature rearrangèd is.
I know not what I think
not having head,
for I pollarded am.

Eyes

Eyes take in the light for hearts to see by.
They are quintessentially the mind's messengers,
barometer of the soul's weather,
and the heart's health.
We tell by the eyes. Looking is the least they do.
When eyes touch others' eyes they sign in.
When it's a stranger in a crowd, on the street,
in a train, and that's all there is of it,
I like to think they are my brother and my sister.
I like to think they are never lost.
God of the one strand of hair, are you also
God of the one look, of the glance, of the glimpse?
I trust one day all will be known
in the deepest bank of the world's meaning
and on that day our eyes will feast.

The Old Ferry

Half in the mud, in the thick of the gulls' squabbles,
an old ferry becomes more and more
what its builders would remember. The square nails
long to be driven home. The prow
can only be imagined now. I embark,
clambering on weather-worn planks.
A child joins me with his questions:
'what is this?' and 'what is that
half-wood-half-iron thing?' We agreed
it was something to do with something else,
possibly the rudder, deep into the mud.
When the bright, new ferry arrived, the child
jumped off his friendly, timbered skeleton,
turned, waved, and called out
a strangely old-fashioned 'goodbye!'
I was left looking into history,
sensing the rain would reveal more grain,
until what once was tree, would, in time, be tree again.

Reflections on Craigie Aitchison's Paintings

1

See,

        a leafless tree
      leaning to the right,
  a fingernail clipping
        moon,
  and Wayney being
      sucked
    upside down
through a thunderous sky
        to Heaven.

2

See,

  people smile in recognition,
     find their friends and point.

3

See,

  the Pope walking in the garden
    in his white soutane
      in the human being stretch of space
        the horizontal band of being us
        with the trees
        the visiting birds
  and the round black papal hat
      cruising in its own air space.

4

See

  the cross, but:

Q. What is the dog doing there?
A. Oh!
  howling beneath the bright cross
  his Master is shining from.

A David Jones Annunciation

In such an ordinary room
the angel came skidding to rest:
she on a bench of prayer
he to get news off his chest.

Arrivals can happen like that
on the day you least expect,
when the washing's on the line
and you've no idea what's next.

He was such a gentle angel
with a lily in his hand,
and his eyes so meekly angled
you has to understand.

The King is in search of a kingdom;
the time to be born is soon,
and God wants you to house him
in the byre of your womb.

She sat as still as the chair
staring at the cool, tiled floor
and the silence was deeper there,
than she'd ever heard before.

Neither knew how to break it.
Neither was wanting to press.
It was probably only a minute
but it felt like an hour to say 'yes'.

'Yes' was the shape of the farmhouse.
'Yes' were the trunks of the trees.
'Yes' was the gate on its hinges.
'Yes' brought the world to its knees.

A David Jones Nativity

(Gentilis animetur)

All four hooves, Welsh as a pony on hill
are inches off the frosted ground. They skip
for a fish tight saviour who is swathed in stillness
between apple breast and pillow of hair.
Come to look at it, all are off the ground:
cow and ladle, shepherdess and lute,
bits of floating Latin, but all stock still,
as if playing statues.

I am waiting for the cockerel to spill
its redness on the page to Botticelli up the colour
and set the world in motion, from out of winter
into summer. Then the snow will melt
and who knows what the sun might loose them into.

Uglow's Nudes

Looking at Uglow's nudes
in the Abbot Hall Art Gallery
what I felt was missing was
the replacing of old breath by new.

So I opened a window and looked
instead at the castle ruin, and thought
of Catherine Parr who wore so many
clothes, including a ruff. I saw a seat too
on the top of the hill and the millennium beacon.

Then I knew as before
that really good paintings
make me want to write poetry.

Pablo Casals plays to the wall

What a fine wall, ancient I would say, of a church,
and the large stone flags are alive with the light
that plays on an old man's bald head.
The head of the cello nestles his neck.
I see his back and his poise.
He plays to the wall, this man
who could fill a concert hall twice over.
He plays, then, for the joy of it, there,
where only the angels come, one
by curious one, stirring the air.

The Piper

It was the relation of bag to pipe
that interested me, like taking
a red velvet pig to market under
your arm: the constant rearrangement
of elbow and finger to accommodate this
live thing. The venue for the night,
the island's ancient lending library,
was in a frenzy. The dusty summer coals
might just have turned to fire.
It took the final tune to reveal
a face made generations ago, when
your grandfather played the same pipes.
The encore set your eyes upon some other island,
on some far distant archipelago.

The Organist's Wrists

Something has to link the brain with the music,
and I think it's the wrists. Wrists put the hands
in the right place, and are the swings for the music
to take flight up to those heart stopping heights,
and back, so your stomach is left where it was,
several feet behind your body. It's the wrists
that hold the fingers to the job, the task
of typing music into living keys.
I've seen how the wrists bring the whole service
to rest, long after the choir have ditched their
cassocks for a smoke and a pint of best.

West Malling Abbey

You know how a moving camera seems
to make the buildings move themselves,
though nothing could be more fixed.
Well, it was like that. I was walking
on a winding path and the tower
and the chapel roof began
to move around themselves, like
a model of the constellations speeded up.
The path and the river at my feet wound
round a different figure of eight,
and I became a dance within a dance,
moving to the sacred space of church.
There we made a circle round the sacrament,
and passed the kiss of peace.
Christ came round in bread and wine,
until all ceased. I could hear my breath
grow quieter in the silence of a little death.
The dance had done its thing.

The Friends' Meeting Room

I have known silences between
breaks in conversation, agonisingly
searching for the next word. I remember
the silence of exams curdling in my stomach;
and the silence of aloneness filled
with small domestic noises,
a kettle clicking off and distant traffic.

I've even known a silence bring me
to my knees, in an ancient church, held
through the regular deep ticking
of a mechanism in the tower
when everything that summer afternoon
had slowed right down. But this,

in a room of many windows
and much light, is another silence
palpable, gathered by life's long haul
attempting to do the right thing,
silence waged with thought, and moral.

Don't

Thank you for that word.
It doesn't frighten or appal me,
just the opposite.
It clears vast oceans of
opportunities away,
and leaves me free,
not to. God or someone or
you need to say it to me
more.

177

A Peculiar Clarity

If I want to hold the silence
to its natural depth, I wait:
wait for the door to bang, the mower
to come to the end of its endless turning,
wait even for clothing to cease to rub
on clothing. Then I wait still more
until the way is clear for the bird
to sing its invisible song,
travelling a long way on the silence,
breaking nothing by its being heard.

Durham Allotments

Professors going to dig their tea
are overlooked in their library of earth
by the Cathedral towers. To me
the whole May scene is held for ever
in a special sort of Saturday afternoon weather.

County Wexford

My shadow lay half the length
of a spinach field. It was that time
of evening, but I turned and walked
back into the sun through the wheat field,
on the tractor tyres' herring-boned path.
Not yet fully ripe the wheat was silver,
like hairs on a summer skin, the whole
swathes of field were smoothed by the wind
stroking the pelt. The wheat succumbed
to the touch as in receipt of gifts. It was then
I noticed other gifts, far off farms in the clefts
of hills, the ascending size of hill to mountain.
In the time it takes for a shadow
to cross a county, I had turned from
onlooker to receiver of bounty.

Skellig Michael: A Pilgrimage

I was on the top of an illuminated wave
the one's you don't believe when you
see them in manuscripts, an upturned 'U',
or on top of a Leviathan, but it was true.
The boat climbed the wave, sat on
top of it, and slid down the other side.
We had the childhood colours too:
blue boat, black sea, white faces.

On arrival the sea doesn't give you up,
but still rolls, and even in your dreams
you will be surging and plummeting,
or leaping off the cliffs like a puffin
which takes a leisurely fifty feet to ease
out of its fall, and tucks its orange feet
behind, and squits its white stuff
like parachutes onto the rocks.

It's only when you leave the lighthouse path
strewn with the skeletons of birds
and thick with a high-pitched smell of bird lime
that you begin to hear the silence
pressing in, far from the engine of the boat
and the orchestrated scream of gulls.

Then the steps begin, the Southern Stairway,
counting six hundred up to an unknown bedroom.
Somehow it felt necessary to be discalced,
my feet, white as a gannet's breast, my boots
hanging round my neck like earrings.
The boatmen I noticed, stayed below.

Rightly, to enter the enclosure you have
to stoop, awkwardly, lowly. You begin by bowing.
In, you cannot see your way out.
The first miracle will be if you're alone,
the second that the sun will shine, the third

that God will talk with you. Pray to St Michael
for three miracles, whose *skellig* it is. Stop.
Breathe. Let in the peace, and if you don't kneel there
where on earth will you kneel?

I looked up and saw an angel standing by the tombs.
She was dressed in brown. She was the guide,
She understood the need for silence.

We can know too much.

This is where the guidebooks stop and the poems begin.
This is where we have to imagine the monks
watching the sky with nothing
between themselves and heaven,
a psalter for food, rain for drink, and possibly
a strip of wheat beyond the enclosure.
This desert is on the edge of the ocean
and they made the edge a virtue.

But surely despair was sometimes the shape
of their beehive hut, a homesickness, when
the elements took leave of God's control
and became something other. Surely, for some,
having said goodbye to the world,
death could not come quickly enough.

A part of us will not come down:
the glimpse of heroism we could never really manage,
a crazy love of Christ, a romance, something
to do with penitence. And as we sit in meetings
in our suits, we'll take the boat again, and climb
with the gulls willing us up further into lightness
for which prayer is the only music, and Christ's coming
the only purpose under heaven.

Night Reaping

It doesn't seem right, but that's
the way it is these days. Through
the bedroom window I see stars in flight
dancing up and down the field,
then realise it's the getting of the harvest in.
Stars are headlights.
They are shaving the land by night.
Falling asleep I realise we haven't
a mythology for this, except a dark one:
the grim reaper comes when we least expect it.
But I bet they don't think of that.
It's a job to do, and when I wake
the field is pitted with new black bales, like
flicked ash, and the reapers are in bed, knackered.

The Funeral

(i.m. William Scammell)

So it was to church that you were brought,
at the end of a long road of Sunday mornings
elsewhere, and friends who didn't think it altogether wrong
to honour you in hard, quiet pews came too.
Most of us were strangers to the place.
One came, who loved you, with only just about
her grieving left, orange flowers held against her womb
like a bridesmaid. The deep, wet grave,
at the edge of the churchyard, looked over fields
to the Solway through a faint December light.

There is a place for such occasions then.
You needed to know that it was there:
this sleeping church, with its
organ pipes and pews, pulpit and stained glass,
and your plot of earth, near where you read and wrote
and smoked, and suffered losses like the rest of us.
To all this comforting and clumsy ritual
death committed you, and by your gracious choice
committed me as well. It was in your will
for me to have the final word. After that, we
gathered round in groups to weep or cry, and hug,
and wonder how or why, to reminisce,
awkwardly, or not, or maybe, without you.

The Massacre of the Innocents

(for Sarah, Jessica, Holly and Milly)

This is the only praying
we can do
for the child beyond the reach of us,
beyond the dental records, and the one shoe.

All that is left us is to pray.
Wing our love to the One
who knows the way,
asking for small acts of kindness to be done.

Praying lets the mind's image
dance beyond the pain,
beyond the anxiety of 'finds',
and out of the reach of the rain.

Michelangelo's Rondanini Pietà

It is all still being made
and it is all just breaking up.
He is being carried, and she
is carrying him now. He is bearing up,
and now is carrying her
in such an awkward verticality:
both so tired, so sad. His work
is done: hers, now over, begins again.
The only hope lies in the spring of
knees, which are broken, but ready
for resurrection. The whole world
is on his back, crying 'now!'

Easter (I)

for they were afraid
MARK 16.8

This Easter I shall paint
the walls a Jerusalem colour:
the green hill, the cockerel's crimson throat,
the purple pillar; and time will
fall into hours, the third, the sixth,
the ninth, into ethereal time.
It could be any time as I walk through town,
sensitive yet unbodied, feeling the weight
of the lowering of Christ, and smelling
the sacrificial hot-cross buns.

Why am I so keen to stay with death
and sorrow, so cautious of the light,
and all that yellowness? I am with the women,
falling off the end of the gospel,
afraid. This year I may learn to fall
and not fear, and find myself lifted
to watch the face of forgiveness rise
with such silence and uncanny grace,
that with the thrush, high in the holly tree,
I will sing, *unique...unique...unique.*

Easter (II)

Easter is never a new thing.
It saw the birth of the whole land,
and is present at each slow spring
of a child's five-petalled hand;

At Easter it is Christ we see,
with his hands at their farthest
stretch, hanging on the axle-tree,
nailed to the east and the west.

Easter comes again, at the sign
of the torn heart, for the saddened
company, and the shrivelled vine –
love all alive on the sudden!

Easter (III)

The empty tomb was like a mouth aghast,
all presence gone and so fast. Only clothes
remained, limp like a broken heart.
It lacked all life, no hope could fill the void,
no clues to follow, or hints to clutch at,
not even angels. I have seen men as such.

Yet as the minutes passed, and the thin light
inspired the sparrows and the larks,
I heard a tune that earlier I was deaf to.
Not too early and not too late, before
the dew had dried and in the length
of shadow and of light, I could believe
the tale before ever I was told.
The tomb was empty but my heart was full.
Love pieced together Christ and made him whole.

Resurrection

I think it took her death to do it.
The light that emanated from the space
she left spoke resurrection.
Who she was took hold of time
and turned it inside out,
and the old laughter which took
such toll of pompous hats and dirgy hymns
was transfigured into something
which got under the skin of suffering
and put it in its place.

So now I tell the secret
that resurrection is the glass
through which we see things differently,
and what was first in the mind of God
becomes the truth at last.

Written in Juice of Lemon

Some poems I write in ink
and they get written with a lot
of furrowing of the brow, and often miss
but some I write in juice of lemon
quickly in my heart
and hope that one day someone's
warmth will iron the secrets into poems
with effortless art.

BEYOND THE DRIFT:
NEW POEMS

(2014)

Left Hand Right Hand

This all emerged because I was too vigorous
with my right hand. My brother was left-handed.
I was right. His hand wrote into ink,
smudging, and I pulled the ink along,
master to the slave, and I was always right,
and he the awkward left, till now.
For I'm becoming left-handed in my soul,
learning to push the pen of knowledge
so it smudges all along the page, unclear,
slow, unsure of what it is to know.
At every word: 'is this the right one?' Beyond
the drift of language I sense a space I am at home in;
which is the mystery of the heart, wordless, patient,
and wrong. Being right seems insufficient now.

The Lakes: A Description
1959

Much of the detail is gone. I could
work it up perhaps, research, but
that might frighten it away. Short trousers
certainly, and a bit of heavy money
in a jerkin pocket. It was the holidays,
for sure; anything not school was holidays.
In the square, near where we stayed,
beside a hotel entrance, but half outside,
was a miraculous shelf of second-hand books.
One only I recall (now lost, long lost, soon lost)
about the Alps. It had maps that concertinaed out
and did the climbing for me. I climbed them
page by page.

Learning the Part

Round and round the school perimeter
I trod the text, imbibing pentameters.
I cursed, I cried, I talked to the trees
as if it had to be out loud to be at all.
To learn the lines was to tell them to the sky,
and plant them in the earth, so they could
grow again in words.

I heard the sound of language as if coming
from the voice that thought it first into a line.
It was as the birds sung it, for nothing
to nothing, to the air, musically.
As Portia pleaded for mercy, I pleaded too.

The tread was all consuming, its sameness
day by day, counting the beats, counting the days,
until the stage would tighten all the words into the heart
and the heart and the text and the tongue took on the part.

In its substance is but air...

The slightest touch
of early evening, hardly air
blows across the harebell
with the mildest wind, such

as if it scarcely had been there.
It touches with the gentlest of puff
where the long, slight stalk
nods 'yes'. Means 'yes'.

This delight, this silent sense of being
is a wonder when you think of wars
and all the clamour of the town,
the mess and all the petty things that grow
into a deep unhappiness.

Yet the harebell calls me to engage with
its mute tolling, its affirming nods,
its delicate openness to blue.

Boarding School

Boarding School happened as two new shoes
relentlessly followed one another onto the train,
going somewhere with a handkerchief,
a cap, and a jar for the newt. The newt
was the last minute thought from the pond
at the bottom of the garden.

We arrived at the place of the making of beds,
up stone steps, and under the high ceilings.
I have no memory so clear as a stranger
turning off the lights.

Searching the geography of the springs
and the thin blanket of the night, I recalled
the newt tucked into the locker, and pondered
the meaning of us not sleeping tight at all.

Today's Inconsequential Stone

How can I describe it?
An inch by inch with one side
rounded, so that it looks like
the letter 'D', and one side of the stone
has the marking of a 'D' on it
which is what I think attracted it to me.

No doubt eventually, it will join
the whole heap of dusty stones
that have been favourites for a day,
yet just for now it reminds me
of the chance beauty of the world
and the size of things you can carry
in your hand, fragments of divinity.

I find a leaf that would lie well on it.
It will lose its yellow beauty
by tomorrow, but today it takes its place
on the grey parchment of stone,
with its unending D-shaped scoring,
soft on tough, light on less light,
leaf on rock, soul on the world's hard core.

Cathedral Evensong, Winter.

It should not do these days, yet it does;
doing the beautiful thing with sparse reward
except to make music for the Lord this afternoon.
Laundry makes a white show of it,
as the sound arrows its way into the dark corners
where they keep the mops and buckets.
We wait the rebound of the chant,
to meet the next lines backing up like waves.
A downy chin suspended on a ruff
covers a deal of stuff like homesickness.
Do they know how good they are, how rare,
and only a handful of us there?

A Bouquet in the Church

The pews were full in the country church
except for a place by me. The handful of believers
waited for their customary Evensong,
and the time was coming for me to start
when in came a girl, not a familiar face,
with a giant bunch of flowers.
It was definitely not a bunch of flowers occasion.
She floated in. She went from side to side
only vaguely searching for a seat.
To her, it didn't seem to matter where she sat,
she had her flowers, and the empty seat
gaped open, close to me. She spotted me,
and came and made a place for flowers
across two kneelers. Evensong became a wedding:
see all the mighty stone had turned to flesh,
and nobody seemed to notice except for me.

On Not Knowing R.S. Thomas

We met over three days
with he being taller and more courteous
than I, and he in a suit.
He came from Rhiw to Torpenhow where
neither place pronounces as it looks,
both hiding, both awkward.
But now it is my turn to visit him.
He long dead, but alive in the Aeolian wind
that finds a way to play
even through the thickest night.
The poem picks up its pace from the seas' drone.
and the not knowing from exactly where
makes hiddenness the glory of it.

Retirement

I'll go into a wood, a barn, a room,
and not come out until my heart
is settled back on God the pivot,
I the balance. A chance for poise
to get my giddy head becalmed
into stillness that absorbs, I wonder what?
Things I dare not write for fear
they might be so, the illness worse,
or better.
I'll enter into converse with my soul
and hope again to learn a love for others,
and of others love for me.
To stop doing one thing, and discover
what refuses to be laid aside.
What keeps compelling me to be attentive?
Nothing new perhaps; just former things
attentively revived.

Driving Home from Basingstoke Crematorium

(i.m. Stan Hughes)

If I had known that as we sang
the final hymn to end your body's stay,
the westward sun outside was fading too,
and turning Dever's stream into a golden way,
I would have added to the tribute then.
So it wasn't till the driving home,
knowing the unimaginable fire had taken you,
that I saw the evening sun contending with the clouds,
and stopped the car. The silence doubled.
I watched the February fire descend
as you became a Mobius twist of gold
gilding the clouds' dull pewter.
As fast as dusk desired to carry you away,
I sensed the eastern dawn would wake, and claim you
for quite a different sort of day.

Knowing too much

In the end, I talked so much about Christ
I wondered if there was any one who
could carry the weight of all that biography.
It all seemed too heavy with expectation
for the lid to rise as lightly as it did.
So now I pause and contemplate
the Magdalen, whose love was heavy
with her news, or wondering as one might,
whether to share it, or to keep it tight.

Evening Light

So it was for this I came away,
to get the long view, free from
what the next minute I'd be late for,
or have no time to finish.
I looked to those immediate brambles,
then over the barbed wire fence
to the tufted fields; and on to an oak wood,
slow to green where nothing moves.
Then further, to where whole woods shrink
to the size of lichen,
and houses and barns huddle
like toys put away for the night.
At this my eyes, hard pierced, seek out
the very edge of sky and land, at its
most distant, soft, and straight geometry.

Give them some poetry

(i.m. Donald Allchin)

1

When first we met I saw a lightness off the ground in him;
the air of outside, high up, the world all sides of us,
had space to breathe the meeting into life.
A meeting that would last both in and out of time,
and all this as I saw it. It may quite well
be fixed inaccurately, but the height and the space
at the first, is sure. He in a cassock. I not.
He just back from America; I coming to the end
of school. I liken it now to other meetings,
other heights, grander and more biblical,
keen not to miss the precedents, and the connections:
Mt Alverna, say, or wherever light takes over from the dark.

2

Of the world he was not; born somehow
to have that extra inch or two which left him in the air.
So many ideas that others could organise,
which they did, and happily, on the whole.
He liked his spirituality corporate;
serving solitaries, he was not one himself.

3

Our common thread was Merton,
that English-American-Nowhereboy. Donald,
returning from Kentucky met the monk
the day that Martin Luther King died,
which left a generation seething, grieving.
I with a volume of some early Merton poems
newly spread with gravy from reading them
at meals and a term away from A-Levels.
From America, Donald wrote about an emptiness
of saints, and of a space unfilled by holiness.

4

Through all the years he came by saints and scholars;
scholars and writers and poets; and religious and hermits,
and poets: and rarely by children, but once he came by Lucy
in her cot, whose heart was not yet strong, and he prayed
and I saw him unusually paternal, and now she bikes up
mountains, and down again, in Wales.

5

And then came Wales for him, and how fresh it looked
upon the page away from English tightness.
He was forever inviting us to 'do Wales',
and got the words from Merton: 'Let's do Wales,' said Merton,
Donald did Wales avidly: so many poets, so many saints,
so many friends. Bardsey, in its distance, in its beauty,
a metaphor for death, for passing from one realm
to another. The journey had begun.

6

The handwriting turned frail.
The phone call said he was enjoying Traherne.
I said,
I was about to conduct a retreat.
He said:
'Give them some poetry.'

Our Unremembered Birth

I've noticed with the dying how skin
tightens on the bone and shines
to something resembling polish.
The eyes shoot out perplexity,
quicker than the hands and feet
do anything.

I've talked about it often enough,
but what will it be like on the instant?
I ask it on a day of sun
in gentle Worcestershire,
as if it could tell me, gently.

Perhaps, like love, knowing
is impossible until it happens;
or like our unremembered birth, hoping
it will emerge in the way we usually
cope with things, as they come.

What's said about death, cannot all be right.
We'll see, or not. So until such time,
I'll leave my death alone a bit
and contemplate the beauty of this tree.

His Laying the Fire

His Laying the Fire

From last night's heat, and on
the faintest glow of the powder's end
of one last dying coal, is a grey memory
of what, if uncontrolled, apparently,
could have ripped through Pudding Lane
and even to the Thames' great wash.
I saw him blow out gently on the residue,
and with just the right amount of air around,
the fire took up its life again.

His rules

Have round you no one in a hurry
or tempestuous, or who has half a
mind on food. They will be divided
in intent. The process is as delicate
as balancing one stone upon another,
or the coal upon the sticks upon the
bow-tie weaving of the *News Chronicle*.

His passing them on

It was as father taught a son.
It is an art as ancient as they come.

Her Sewing

trailing the thread
with thinnest of cottons
walking it blindfold
so it bumps into jugs
wrapping round wood
like weed in the tide
like lines in the sand
stitching up opposites
forward and further
backwoods and sideways
who would have thought it
any-way-up-side
watching my mother
darning the socks
sewing the name tapes

Marriage

Marriage, like sport, and much else too,
is like the weather, and to judge success
if we can talk like that, is knowing
in particular weathers how to dress.
In storms about the keys, we become
like macs and boots and greatcoats, buttoned tight;
while on the rare good days of summer sun
we dress right down as angels in the light.
So marriage can become the unseen atmosphere
in which we remain ourselves, together.
Despite the sudden fears and tears,
love remains our general weather.
It's not that we can do it well, but rather
what we let love do to us, that tells.

Angel of the North

This angel is not the friendly one who slipped into
Mary's kitchen, and brought good tidings;
nor the one who fed Elijah
in the wilderness with cakes;
nor the one who makes discreet and
timely re-arrangements to the laws of nature,
turning rain into sunshine just for me;
nor the affectionate side of a lifetime's love
whose sacrament is remembering special days;
nor the children in the nativity play, turning
tinsel and silver paper into star and halo.

This angel rolled out on its back
from the last proud shipyard and was lifted
up, in iron boots to be a boast, a folly,
something we never could imagine as it lay
horizontal in the burning fiery furnace
with Shadrach, Meshach, and Abednego.
This angel rose with Sopwith Camel wings
and only then was told its job was not to fly.

Perhaps it was the bird circling round its head,
or the empty goal posts in the field behind it,
or the man with the pit-bull terrier among the daisies
and the dandelions, or all the dead lying underneath
the hill, that jump-started me to tears.
Let's just say one day an angel found its feet
and stayed, to test the unangelic years.

Dusk

The bird on the top branch is singing.
I am held by it as the dusk begins to cloak
the valley, and the bird breaks into evensong.
I can see scissors silhouetted as a beak
against the fading light, smoothing out the day
into dusk. Dusk has a different stillness to the dawn.
People are finding doors to shut,
news to watch, curtains to draw,
leaving the bird the whole last bit of sky
to sing in. The sound, as much sweet sucking in
as ringing out, is one voice and one reply
where song and night-time meet.
I look away and miss its flight, but the branch
for a moment bounces and bounces its good night.

Gertrude Jekyll's Lindisfarne Garden

Having visited the Island in the mist
when grey was the only dishcloth
to damp the ground and wipe the sky
of all its light, I could not have imagined
this; but now I see gold; and next to gold
orange, then some yellow, cream too,
then butter the colour it used to be,
and bridal white. Letting myself for once
enjoy the pinks which went from darker
to vivid crimson to purple. And still around it all
under the grey-filled sky, by the rocks,
this garden is planted, a plot in a wilderness,
where colour seems the only answer to
the questions, how and why and for what.

An Edwardian Conversation with a Harebell

I ask about the bells of Notre Dame
and those in Florence and the Tower of Pisa,
and of single bells, and how the shape is all the same
and how I wish that I were wiser in the case of flowers
especially in the telling of their names.

I count you: five of stamens, five of petals
as the Reverend Keble Martin taught;
but theologically you are fragile,
as Saint Matthew said, held by such
a thin campanile, and always
seemingly, only just about to ascend.

The day I came and you, my fragile bell, had gone,
a family opened up its picnic on the spot.
I took my place a little distance off;
and I was well aware that
you were no more to be seen,
and you, unaware that I had ever been.

Water

It only takes a stone of magnitude
to steer the water round both sides,
and let a flow that falls and spreads
where sound is heard before it's seen;
and what I need is to forget
what poetry books have said
and let our own remembrance
pin the beauty of the liquid measure down.

The spate of winter has left thumps
of broken branches which stuff the beck,
so it's hard to see the water, but I can hear it:
a tenor register of liquid clumps
are urgent to be on. I can see the silent
movement of what's to come
through the play of light upon it.
Only the smallest bits of petal show
its movement. None of this was grand,
but it stopped me to note the sounds
so that they trembled, and worried themselves
into a root and fell, until
the next great rains would come.

Today, there is no menace at all.

St Herbert's Isle, Derwentwater

Island of the wild garlic
Island of the brooding geese
Island of the fallen oaks
Island of the birds in chorus
    of the lapping water
    of the sun on my page

Island of the mossy shore
Island of the stone pillow
Island of the spiritual friend
Island of the British trees
    of the roots above ground
    of the spider on my page
    of the manuscript heads of ducks

Island without ice cream
Island without notices
Island to kiss the ground of
Island to make decisions in
Island of the geese trumpeters
    of the beetle on the leaf mountain

    where oak trees grow out of oak trees
    where Bede is still read

    soft island, safe island,
    Island where you've not seen it on a bad day

    St Herbert pray for us
    St Cuthbert pray for us
    the author of the 'Anonymous
    Life of Cuthbert' pray for us

    Not that it was easy for them.
    It brought Herbert to the bone of endurance.

Island of the ministry of angels
Island of a lonely death
Island of a glorious resurrection.

In Praise of the Oak Tree

When you were a sapling oak, I imagine
Wordsworth completing a skate run
on the frozen tarn beside you.
Now you are a great tree,
thirty feet across and twenty high.
We gaze at your mansions, yawnings,
stretchings, and see goblins in the twists.
I browse a metaphor of life through you.
You resemble everything that grows
and yearns for an ever longer reach.
Reaching is what you seem to do best.

The Book of Wings

The Convent garden is a place apart,
and the Sisters were at Prime or somewhere else,
so I had the whole long stretch of bedding plants,
flowers, and vegetables, to be alone among.

I could drift like the Cabbage White
which was reading its book of wings,
now open, now shut; now open again,
flitting here and there, and back again.

A chromium disc hangs sentinel among the beans
attempting to scare what largely isn't there
on this windless of days; so it's the slightest of drafts
that carries the thistledown across the garden
to wherever it may end, secret, silent, and wayward.

Yet, what is this? The coolness of a fox
padding its path on the very boundary of its menace?
I hold my breath to see what that can reek.
He stops, he turns, he does whatever word for menace
does; and takes the path which monarchs spy, grateful
to be within the safe chaotic sphere of butterflies.

Diving

The mist on the lake
with its muffled light
of pewter and beaten
silver, means I sense it
more than see it. Out of
the many ducks, this one
on its wheel of prayer
dives from water to
water, through air. It
knows what its beak
can do. I wish I could
do what I have to do
like you with ease and
meaning, in the boundary
of my mind and body.
Be what I was meant
to be, without wings,
from the beginning.

Green

Colour spurs us to philosophise
WITTGENSTEIN

I never did think grass was just a plant,
but saw it more like custard,
or a towel, something that got rolled out
for lazing on before exams; part of the English kit.

But now in these green days
when grass is more political,
I rather long for it to be a species
and get in close to it with spectacles.

So on this upland grass of Dorset
I wonder how it is that we see green
as green? What process sets
the green in motion, as something known and seen?

I notice how the colour changes with the break
in cloud; or, which edge of the green shoot
shows most green; or, how it weathers into the light
or away; or how the green sheath

is caught by the light, or not, or stays its dull reverse;
or, what the yellow cowslip has to say
to blend the greenness down a shade, when it converses
in a 'hello, how are you?' sort of way.

Green doesn't advertise itself,
except to the sun. Its secret is hidden,
but it can surprise you,
becoming 'all green on the sudden'.

I think of Mendel, Bateson, Crick,
each surpassing the other in theories;
their models ever more tree-like,
taking over the laboratory.

But for most it's 'Green grow the rushes O',
and here's to the grass, and the grass to us,
along with the nappies on the hard shoulder,
scattered by the whoosh of the motorway bus.

In the end, how we see the green shoots
depends on what we know of green,
which depends on how much is left to be seen
when we've poisoned all England to its roots.

Entering Eden

How I know I'm back in Eden is when
the hills make curious bubblings-up.

How the growl of a light aircraft dies away
leaving the skylark's chatter on the late March air.

How the long turned earth waits, one side dark,
one side light, for the receiving of the seed.

How this place manages to hold its memories.

How I think the birds know I'm back.
How I hear them, though my ears are not yet tuned.

How my neck has not stretched high enough
but is too much bent on earth.

How bees move wisely,
How I love to hear the skylark sing:
How the place is made for praise.
How it is meant for the ascription of glory.

The Narrow Window

Whoever thought to make this window
had more than light in mind,
and yet the light is what a window's for
and the window nothing in itself
but to let this nothing to and fro.

The window and the light are nothing
except the viewer makes it so
and a viewer nothing without a view.

Window, light, view and viewed,
all stop at the apple tree,
leaning from the east, smoothing the blush
of an autumn cox against the green.

Four Gardens

The Garden of Eden

Somehow emblematic;
more talk than weeding;
a disaster reverberating;
just the one tree, and
no flowers, at least
none that I could see.

Abbot Mendel's Garden
(1822–1884)

O! what tension there was
      between
  Prime and *Vespers*
  Vespers and *Statistics*
  Statistics and *Biology*
  Biology and *Darwin*.

The bees of course understood,
and Mendel understood the bees,
and the bees liked the way
Mendel had structured their hives.

Walafrid Strabo's Garden
(800–849)

There are still gardeners
among the lettuces this hot day
when the backs of the monks
are bent to the sun; hoe, scrape lean, pick...
hoe, scrape, lean, pick, hoe, scrape...
The lettuces make long widening stripes
of maroon and green, dark and light
just as the colours of the painted arches
of his church. The same sun and rain
brought more than vegetables to ripeness.

The Rectory Garden
(2000)

Not my garden really, rather,
generations of clergy long before me
leading up to the annual Garden Party.
The roller hasn't done a day's work in years,
but once in the year for tea and cakes
we have a particularly fine setting
for Evensong, and play the
Edwardian game with grace
and the neighbours seem not
to complain; at least not face to face.

The Beck

I am amongst the liquid sound of water
over stone. Don't imagine cataracts; but
think rather music that is more liquid than
traffic's incessant thrum, relentless
in its desire to tumble; passionate
to search for what is level, what is home.
The orchestra, liquid in its tumbling
responds to the rocks by escaping down,
down into a froth of falling, taking its nifty
cut-through, over rock and into pool.

A string of pearls has come adrift,
washed from pool to pool, down, all the way down
until summer dries the hillside to a dribble,
leaving only the sound of the sheep's nibbling.

Squirrel

I see the squirrel bounce the trees,
nimble in its getaway.
Such is its territory, its range.
It is the cowboy of all it sees.

I watch it run a whole parade of oaks
from top of branch to trunk and on,
assured of expertise in its swift world,
with never a need to coax. It is just done.

Fixed I am at the window, amazed,
at the route it runs, like water, on and on,
pressing through a pipe to appear
with its nut and its nibble, then gone.

Soil

This soil must be somewhere in my blood,
a sediment laid down within my roots.
I feel comfortable with it, don't mind it
through my fingers, on my boots.
Occasionally, some of the hardest stones
I keep, to touch, to hold down flighty papers,
sometimes sermons, but most likely just to own.
In the narrow lanes I trace the seams of soil
from inside the window of the bus.
Further into town I see only buildings,
and sense a loss. Something about the feeling
of the soil is most particular for us.

Considering the Birds

Such anxiety the birds have not:
of wrestling with the day to come,
of things that might be ghosts
that former teachers summon.
How fears hold sway for us
even on the brightest day,
yet such things the birds do not perceive,
else I think they would not sing that way.

Giverney in May

I imagined heat oozing from petals
but it was cold. A man in orange
was sawing a headache into a tree.
Cameras were doing all the remembering,
but redemption came with a child, her nose
in a tulip's nose. I woke to the old vision
of *people, as trees walking*, and nature,
knowing no irony, deserved no condemnation.

The Slicing of Carrots

Legs tucked satisfactorily under her
she was at ease with the stone floor.
For most it was the time of resting.
The still kitchen hung in the balance
of the day. The light was pressed
through only one of the doors,
the other being shut. I could see
the slicing of the carrots produced a pile
of saffron-coloured shards. Light
and dark seemed more so and tighter
for being opposites. The shot-through silk
of her sari, and the shape and rhyme of the duty,
seemed right for one content to work.
The peace that came with the soul of the place
in which it was done, shared her beauty.
Beauty and light seemed something
she both wore, and won.

The Village Potter, Karnataka

He is himself his trade.
The life and work are one.
Dyed and drenched in clay,
pot and skin share the same colour.
The same as makes the pot
the same makes him.
Sitting on the earth
his livelihood spins round
close to his navel and his birth.
He spins the wheel faster
until with casual grace,
the time has come
to throw the clay
precisely
onto the central place.

The Dunnabeck

(i.m. Robert Woof)

It began with that picture by Haydon
of Wordsworth in the beck
standing on a rock, thinking through one arm
held at the elbow, indicating
a longish pose. I don't mean any irony.
I like it. I like it intensely because
I would naturally do the same but quicker
for fear of being observed, or snapped into
conversation by 'do you live round here?'

I wander from rock to rock remembering
Robert and thinking what he will be now:
part of the great everything perhaps,
or particular in some particular way
to do with what mattered to him.
And not just books, but his genius
of engaging one with another.

Then there were the rocks, the water and the air,
and the way they speak the truth just enough
and automatically, like the space above,
and all that ragged, shabby clothes stuff...

How the Opposites Conjoin

(for Peter and Elizabeth Fisher)

Of our group, you went the first.
No sooner done with finals
than something newer
was on the syllabus. A rival

attraction, like the River Wear winding
your hearts round each
other, and joining
a ministry and a marriage.

The same old comfortable stuff was shifted
from Bedford, to Guildford, to Lincoln.
from youth club to students,
and then north to Houghton-le-Spring.

Penultimately, surprisingly, parts of Birmingham
and its responsibilities, and now to this church
making the tour complete,
as you welcome us to this anniversary
with grandchildren at your feet.

I like the photographs in the order of service.
They tell a story:
from wedding nerves to 'love-in-a-mist',
a progress of glory.

What else then for a wedding poem,
which is not lush, or out of place,
untrue, or overblown? Perhaps
something on intimacy and space;

or on how the opposites conjoin
when marriage, like the Pyrenees,
bring France and Spain
into the one accommodating piece.

The sort of person she is

(for Vicky Darling)

She will pick flowers early,
quickly, this one, this one, and this one;
a swift bend of the stalk to breaking
and another bloom joins the bouquet,
and, oh yes, that one too. There is a towel
on her arm and her hair is lank
from the swimming earlier. So the damp
of the dew and the pool and the wash and
all that shakes from the flowers is the sort of
spray you might expect from a wedding day,
and not just any old Thursday, which it is.

A Thank-you Letter for a Shell

Dear Pippa,

Alas! It took me seconds to drop your slippery,
completely ungraspable shell of a birthday present.
I tried. I clipped on my 'Iron-Grab-it-Hand'
to pick it up again, but it slipped away
homesick for its rock-pool. It was however
beautiful none the less: a curl within a curl,
a whorl, a globe, a bowl, a boule...
but there I fear it will stay, until
it secedes from the alliance of
all the other beautiful, small objects,
which have but a fleeting play-time;
casualties of loss, drying into drabness,
ennui, or just life's hostage to the hoover
fouled up half-way into a non-rhyming line;

Forgive me.

A Seat in the Transept

(i.m. Michael Mayne)

The slant November sun sought out
details that might normally be missed:
a quiff of hair roughed up from pulling off a hat
as we stepped, late into the cathedral's light.
Our seat was beside a recumbent knight,
his gauntlets clamped in prayer,
the sun in shafts fingering the armoury:
the breastplate, and the helmet there.
The morning sun seemed to caress
a familiar body for the final time.

Since we were some distance from the coffin
this effigy became a metaphor. It seemed
the internecine wars that thrust your body through
and through, were ready now to undress
your soldiery, and make once more all air of you.

St Columba, an Elegy

He was wise about angels.
He gleaned among the psalms.
He read the books that Cassian read.
He won battles with his gluttony.

He wrote the harmony of the course of the moon,
the course which it ran with the rays of the sun,
and with the course of the sea.

He was holy. He was chaste.
He loved the Books of Solomon.
His skill in priestly matters was unique.
He died in the cause of good sense,
but for the rest there is slim evidence.

Sheila Fell, Cumberland Artist

I remember the fateful day she
tumbled down her London stairs
and the news took no time to reach
the Grafton Gallery, and then reverberate
north to the stern and silent hills.

Now the time it would have taken
to live her life again, sees the paintings
return to a northern gallery. So what?
It is the renunciation of the word
that seems uppermost in the silence now.
As if there was a self imposed embargo
on any sound at all. The lips of the paint
are sealed in some secret that she keeps.
The shapes renounce all sound.
The gallery is a church of deep-set hills,
with men returning home
and clutching all the secrets tight
as they lift, and then let go, the latch.

Tennyson's Troubles

(for the Speddings of Mirehouse)

Tennyson, in throes of some distress
with Hallam dying, was much aware
that all those larger themes
they looked to share together
were seeming frail,
with little time to be expressed
or most, to be resolved.

The Poet's hat, his cape, his curls,
his stick, the outward him
belied what churned
the ocean of his mind within.

So with his heart beset by Troy
and drawing from the whole
of all that fed his mind just then,
it was his 'Ulysses' that brought
the inspiration up from Hallam's grave
and set the laurels free
to work his poetry.

Hopkins' Last Words

There is something in me likes the deep
secret library of his soul, that searches
dialect from every skipping syllable
and abrupt enjambment, like the one
skate on the bow bend, dug firm
to an abrupt and showering full stop.

What was the pull or the draw or the need
that sent me as soon as I could to the shops
to get W.H. Gardner's *Selection of Hopkins'*
Prose and Poetry and to find a feast of words,
kicking to and fro in the joy and the gloom?

Hopkins, aware that his cough was not going away
took his penultimate poem from the scriptures,
working a piece of Jeremiah, which, through it's dark
encasement, brought Hopkins completely
to himself. It is not known who caught
the final words that hung upon a wing,
but someone must have heard
and taken them to heart, and let us know,
that for three final electric times the poet
was heard to say, 'I am so happy, so happy, so happy.'

John Donne's Shroud

That familiar frontispiece of withered face
surrounded by a waterfall of shroud
tied at the top so prettily, confronted me.
It was on a morning walk up Dunnabeck:
the water tumbling down in moderate spate
divided by a jutting rock, revealed his smile,
his coin-closed eyes. The water tumbled bridal
round the leathered cheeks, and then for miles
and miles of millinery, God's secretary
was unwound into death's expansive sea.

Canon Fenton, Theologian

There was something defiant about his funeral,
as if he had decided from the start
to resist the eulogy.

No one more fascinated than he
by the ending of St Mark's Gospel,
refusing the milliner's itch, to stitch
just one more bit onto the story.
For him the story was of faith,
and how faith narrows down the power
of most things, this side of the future.

The eulogy would be merely what he did
in the waiting room: life's see-sawing
of one foot onto the other, which is
nothing, in comparison to the light
so bright we can only see it
through the negative. That is the light
that brooks no eulogy.

The outer life is burnt or buried on a particular date,
but faith flies away from there, to become something
suddenly other. No one I know has been so firm on that.

Miss Taylor, Church Organist

This little bird with wings of steel
stopped me in my tracks at a single glance,
as birds do when they land for just a second
on the table spread with crumbs. For crumbs
read quavers, semi-quavers, minims:
she knew them all, flew down upon them
with organist's feet which do such clever
things in opposite directions needing
two parts of the brain to work together.
Sometimes, when it was winter she wore
a mohair coat and mittens, which
did the business of the skin to keep her warm.

We will tell the story of the parking of her car
in the living room, until we lose our breath;
or die of the pain of laughing:
Meanwhile it remains an image of defiance,
the Lancastrian red-rose to the death.

What she would really like, would be to rise up
from the organ pit at the Saturday film matinee
and play *Jerusalem*, and then just keep going until
she and the white painted organ ascend, like Elijah,
into heaven, which she did in her way.
For back with her sister, they may play duets,
and heaven will be them both, at their musical best.

Bowes Churchyard, Early Morning

I was early morning browsing
and came across a churchyard
with this inscription:
'Here lies Catherine, the daughter of the Reverend...'
and that was all, for the ancient moss had had its say,
obliterating all the rest of what may well have been
a longer tribute as in Victorian times.
So all I had to go on was a glimpse
of part of the end, of a part of a name,
the relation to your father
and all that could be conjured from your being
in this quiet and lonely place the *'Daughter of the Reverend'*.

A sparrow wheeled from headstone to headstone
cutting through the morning sun.
A thrush pushed its speckled chest into a scuttle
through the damp grass.

'Daughter of the Reverend...' it kept coming:
and all that responsibility in the eyes of the parish,
all that love, all that guilt that fathers and daughters
leave sometimes to brew in a Rectory.

The dustbin men had left the engine running.
The emptying of bins, chugs and clumps
and slams beside the churchyard wall,
blocking any passing sentiment.

Catherine, daughter was your vocation
and I think of your father, the Reverend,
devastated. The tombstone hints at that.

Yet I must uncurl from this damp section of a wall,
and return to a less unreal world; yet some things,
however distant seem never quite to leave at all.

Together: An Elegy

His Honour Judge Derek Stanley

Struggling to know who to be,
formed in fear and crudity,
you held to the stature
that carved out a moral future,

while we were floundering. How,
over and over again I play that slow,
flickering, too sudden clip of film
of five years in the same tight realm,
learning to be grown up this and that.

You turned out in wig and bands,
I in belt and fraying cassock.

But it's not for the gear I catch myself
doing these extraordinary dry hiccups of tears,
tears of 'it could be me, but it's you'. Tears
deeper than those we both cried down a bed
into thin pillows, half through pity, half fear.

You went your way. I went mine,
but what tied us then, ties us still
through the memory of voice and place;
using words we never would have thought to say
then, but which both of us came to know,
like love, like grace.

Josephine Butler walks the streets

We notice first her clothes, the bustle,
the black, leaving only the skin of her face
bone china. The rest is passion and rustle,
constantly awake to sin
and the vision of woman's bodies,
wrecked under duress from the Garrison.
She walks late along Hope Street
gathering such a one back home;
not for the first time, or the last,
to die within the scent of gardenias,
and between clean sheets.

The Christ Child in a Flemish Landscape

Saviour of the world,
wherever the sails turn on the windmill
and the rivers run between banks
then disappear; where a pedlar
sets off early with his tied pack
on a long stick over his shoulder,
and a hat; there you sit on your mother's lap,
noiselessly weighing the world
to a poise.

The Annunciation of the Blessed Virgin Mary

And the Angel came in unto her
from a painting by Sophie Hacker

Like an artist, she was always seeking
to make more room for light, and from herself
abandon all that blocked the strange bright thing.

It came as fire and moon and stars at night,
and touched by brightness she saw the dust ignite,
dancing in shafts of geometric light.

She read by it. It was the silent parable
on her skin. The texts were named in turn
as the shadow moved through the slow room.

Then came the day that Gabriel called her name
and to the light she swirled. Then wordless both,
the light enclosed her, and she all light became.

The wonder; for what before had never
been, never inched so close
to any human being, was done for ever.

Crucifixion, 1926

(from an engraving by David Jones)

What a long time it's been since the stable.
The good ship sailed without a mariner.
Cain took a sword to his brother Abel,
as the sun sank down and the cross rose higher.

Between he and she, and that and this,
no end of writhing under the ground.
Ass-head and dragon lick the spilled chalice,
as the cross rose higher and the sun sank down.

St John on tiptoe lifted the flowers.
All three women came up from the town.
Who could have imagined three such long hours
as the cross rose higher and the sun sank down.

Good Friday and the Magnolia Tree

Good Friday has blown stark away
with the last of the spirit's puff
and the final hymn over and done.
Heavy with a death, I come out of church
smack into the full shopping sun.
Inside, so much talk of dark;
outside, the first ice cream of spring
is being licked under the magnolia tree
by two lover's tongues simultaneously.
Not that I would have it any other way,
for Christ's tree also blossomed as he hung.

One of the Wise Men

(from a pastel by Craigie Aitchison)

one of the Wise Men
one of the three
his coming in
his entry into
the way his sandal was coming in
how his head inclined a little
how his nose inclined as well
how the right hand held a gift
how the right hand held a box
how the box was offered up
how the left hand held his robes down
how the right hand held the box out
how the memory stays so still

Love's Aerial Feasts for ordinary days

This poem started out by our walking up 'the Dixon Heights'
with long-term friends. The air was more above us
than below; and for April, unusually still.
We were talking weddings, and of the glory of the view;
(and I had promised you a poem
and the days that were left were few.)

The heights of hills can bring sublime exchanges,
like songs of love with wonder in their dreams.
We reached the summit of our climb
as if heaven was only one final step away
and such I thought must be the glory of this wedding day.

Let there be no 'ifs or buts' about it;
the complementary glory of the lower ground
is not better, is not worse, than the glorious height.

Our walk led briskly to a long descent, and we were
grateful to be nearer home and back on level ground.

This brings me to the title of the poem
'Love's aerial feasts for ordinary days'
which makes a Monday rich with Sunday's sounds
and turns each day into a holy day where Love abounds.

George Herbert and the Clergy Meeting

His sock was twisted and the world
was not yet saved. To uncurl the sock
took energy that fast revealed
the problem was not the sock, rather

a sudden lack of smoothness
felt along the nerves. The day
had the potential to distress
his best intentions, come what may.

Today, he thought, I'll walk along the river.
The sun is out; spring
has come, I'll make a joy of it,
and 'be anxious for nothing'.

The ducks were kneading down their nests.
The stream ran close upon its bed.
The swallows dipped and swooped with zest,
and there, the place he once fell in the mud.

Ah well, arriving among those who easily
could sap him like the desert sun,
the walk continued in his soul,
and he found a way to reach each one.

The Awe that Falls on Language

Words are hiding somewhere inaccessible.
They are not coming when I call.
They are around, I see them hovering
on the tip of the tongue
but that's where it stays, shut.
There is an awe that falls on language.
Perhaps the time is not yet right;
like Zechariah waiting for his new born son
for whom he had no words.
God took his time to present the child,
and for the bell and tongue to be unstrung.

In Praise of the Convent Cart

There is something about its thin frail wheels
its back-street bonfire night engineering,
and the 'Donkey Derby' faithfulness of its appeal
that makes it, of its type, an almost perfect thing.

Known as 'Le Cadillac' in the Convent, it brings
food in towelled pots, and could not be simpler.
It has irony and beauty, and its steering
is the gift of the wind in a full-sail wimple.

The Cuff-links and the Cockermouth Floods

There was a man who had a shop
on the south side of the street,
with lots of useful things, like cuff-links, in it.
I bought two pairs and since have lost one half of each.
I hope the shop has been restored: but
I wonder. It would take some filling up again with stock,
when such a wild and ruthless sweeping came again
that night-and day-and night, shops neither open nor shut.
I saw it on the News in safety: the boats, the sand-bagging,
the terrible fear and sense of loss
of all that had been built, then tossed
into a muddy, swirling torrent, unregarding.
I have two different halves of cuff-links bought from you,
and wear them. It's all that I can think to do.

Allhallows Church

A Dream

It was just another day on which
the pew-length spaces filled the church,
one person here, another there, equal
but opposite in their accustomed place.
Nothing much distracted from routine
turnings of the page. We were content
to limit things to what we had the breath for
until, counting out the bread, I looked
and saw the church was full of people:
all alert and tall and ready.
Some long dead had now returned to sing,
some recent friends, all light and shining
in the latticed sun. I could not move
for those that loved the place.
They needed welcoming, and so I stepped
beyond the rubrics, and said my stumbling piece:
'what threadbare hosts caught unexpectedly,
how they had as much a right as we,
how valued for their clothes of white and gold
and pale green'. Only half remembering
the wedding and the flowers that just
the day before had been arranged,
with never this in mind.

The Lanercost Poems

In 1306, Edward I had his final stay with his court at Lanercost Priory. Built with stone from Hadrians Wall, it lies beside the River Irving close to Brampton. 700 years later in 2006 Prince Edward was invited to a commemoration and this poem was written for that occasion.

Mattins 1.30 A.M.
A Drawing from the Lanercost Cartulary

We begin with the black-robed Canon
who flies, either upwards, tonsure first,
or gently downwards from heaven
past the left hand edge of a charter
that confirms the rights of canons
to elect their own Prior.

We begin with the Canons
for they were the first to come,
but not the last to go from this place.
They had their time. It was enough:
too much rampaging all around them
was unconducive to Augustine's retiring life.

Mary Magdalene high up in the rose-cheeked stone:
   pray for us.
Augustine, of the Rule:
   pray for us.
Canon in black, airborne,
in your wide-sleeved rochet:
   pray for us

Lauds 1.45 A.M.
The Rule of St Augustine

Let us be monastic too,
honed to be the prayer in all we do.
To build a life upon a rule:
unfashionable but real.
We beg an inward bell to ring,
which brings to each small act
the notion of remembering.

Prime 7 A.M.
A Canon reciting Prime falls asleep and dreams

During Prime I go for a walk, in my head.
The sun is still at the bottom of the hedge.
The birds are busy, if not with prayer
then with singing. I pass the byre,
and there is more singing, maybe humming,
no, whistling, from the cowman.
I see only the crusted blade of the shovel
in and out of the door, in and out
pushing dung towards the slurry,
and with that, Prime is done. So soon.

Terce 9 A.M.
The East Window

If we could only see through glass
(so even sweet George Herbert disappears)
and then persist in looking,
till the eye can pass through stone
and then through air.

Then the eye within the heart
will see things as they are,
and well supplied from there,
returns (as good George Herbert did)
with only 'praise' identified.

High Mass 10 A.M.
Edward 1 at Lanercost

Into this persistent rhythm rode a king
whose many strengths had left him weary,
and age and death, which conquer everything
had brought him to an unarranged frontier.

What it must have been to be a king, when power,
crown, sword, and mace, were more than metaphor.
He knew their clash and smell, 'their finest hour',
and worst. Each day he must have dressed for war.

When the border of mortality
closed in on him, and he failed to take Scotland
by the skirts, he turned with unusual frailty,
and spiralled down upon the dangerous sands.

Noon. Dinner, followed by work in Winter and sleep in Summer
A Fantasia on a Page of Pevsner, or, The Army Comes to Town

I make for the town to see the girl who's sitting on the wall biting her
fingernails waiting to be noticed. A lad stabs three fingers in the air and
couldn't care a dog's tooth for very much. He's over-active in his hood-
mould. His mates: the tie beams, the kingposts, the two-way struts, and the
raking queenposts are urgent, but about nothing. They spin, and wheel, and
cry holla.
    Watch out, history! That man has the teeth of a dog.

Evensong 4.30 P.M.
A Walk by the River Irthing

Saying simple things, like fishing,
water, bridge, washing, cart:

at times that's all our mind will let us say:
things like, 'I'm going for a walk,

wander about, sit on a stile, pick up a stone,
look into the river, throw something in, come back.'

Not spiritual at all, until you think:
fishing, water, washing, cart.

Compline 6 P.M.
Sitting on East Turret 52A

Christ enters the human frontier,
on an evening when the sun
          is still not tired at supper time,
and a single car is all that's left
of a traffic jam. A dog barks,
a sheep cries, the car door shuts,
and gradually the sound on the A69
is turned right down.

Nine Lessons and Carols;

A Theological View

Every Christmas I wish St John would come
and read the final lesson for himself.
Then I could listen for his run of syllables;
his subtle language, the changes solved.

I'd hear his tone of voice; watch his eyes,
anything that could expose reality
and help the statutory feasting time
of Christmas, unfold more naturally.

I might, seeing him there, understand this word,
who is The Word. How it might mean something
that cuts as deep as any sword; yet
is the source of life, life's truth, its meaning.

And would John be surprised
by the words St Matthew wrote and set beside
John's Greek: words we know quite well
like stable, baby, straw, and star,
none of which St John had wish to spell.

So we are left to wonder in the annual rush,
whether one can be resolved into the other,
all swaddled somehow into the hush of a manger:
with both light, and child, and mother.

Tintern Abbey

There is a place for ruins
depending usually on the amount of draught.

Today my diagram tells me
south is in collusion with the sun
so I can dawdle, go slowly
with the heel going gently down before the toe
right along the central aisle.

The guidebook's good, but there is still
quite some imagining how the normal
things of life, especially those in latin,
might actually have felt with all this stone about.

Yet in the garden, surrounded
by uneven walls and tall woods,
here is still the place to put aside
The Guide however good,
and not to be concerned
about anything very much at all.

Astley Church

I love the summer stillness of this Church,
which has little to do but live through time,
to the chime of bells which ring all round
to east and west calling us to search inside.

Like Larkin, I leave the door ajar,
and in the summer let loose a shining
set-square of light along the floor
and enter into an ancient sense of awe.

Lying in the chancel are the Blounts.
They are quiet too and have been,
since the ruffs and gauntlets and slippered feet
were upward turned toward the beams.

It's time to let some feeling pray in me,
which is best done by doing nothing well,
which means simply handing over things
to the one who knows, and let it be.

Leaving exerts in me a mild shock of sun,
but steadied, I drift towards a poet's grave
for its memory and its dust. Frances Havergal
was daughter of the vicarage, when days went slow

which leaves a moment for the finding of her grave
in the longish grass, beside the tree
and a chance to recall but not I fear to sing:
'Take my feet and let them be
swift and beautiful for thee.'

An Afternoon Walk

I've been following wild garlic
round all my life, on river banks,
with the river deepening its bed
lifting up the sandstone layers,
     and with the falling the rising
     and with the rising the deepening.

And are the celandines both yellow
and white in among the nettles?
And is that blossom on the ground
just two heads? Take me to the
tree you came from just now
your stamen freckled blossom,
your bees' food.

I might have expected the blossom
but not this welcome. Such
a crowded beauty, a bee
might not know where to begin.
Even the trunk leans with its
lightweight load, blushing
against the dark yew of the churchyard
backed by hill upon hill.

In the empty church,
the patient mechanism
of the clock, ticks

     back,
     forth,

     back,
     forth

     back…

The Fly and the Prayer

It is nothing much, but when you
have settled into prayer, found the space
early, the house asleep, and you are
all set to welcome the Almighty, and a fly
from nowhere begins to flit, and then
sets off an irregular buzzer: do you
say 'amen' and give up,
or incorporate it?

INDEX

Index of titles

Printed in the USA
CPSIA information can be obtained
at www.ICGtesting.com
JSHW082227140824
68134JS00016B/773

9 781780 371047